THE AUTHENTIC MARKETER

(Book 1: Live)

THE AUTHENTIC MARKETER

(Book 1: Live)

The Real Girl's Guide to Know Your Worth, Get More Clients & Grow a Business that Genuinely Fits Your Lifestyle

LINDA BASSO

BIG MOOSE PUBLISHING

Copyright ©2020 Linda Basso

Published by: Big Moose Publishing
PO Box 127 Site 601 RR#6 Saskatoon, SK CANADA S7K3J9
www.bigmoosepublishing.com

All rights reserved. No part of this book may be used or reproduced by any means, graphic, electronic, or mechanical, including photocopying, recording, taping or by any information storage retrieval system without the written permission of the author except in the case of brief quotations embodied in critical articles and reviews.

Because of the dynamic nature of the Internet, any web addresses or links contained in this book may have changed since publication and may no longer be valid. The views expressed in this work are solely those of the author(s) and do not necessarily reflect the views of the publisher, and the publisher hereby disclaims any responsibility for them.

The author(s) of this book does not dispense medical advice or prescribe the use of any technique as a form of treatment for physical, emotional, or medical problems without the advice of a physician, either directly or indirectly. The intent of the author is only to offer information of a general nature to help you in your quest for emotional and spiritual well-being. In the event you use any of the information in this book for yourself, which is your constitutional right, the author and the publisher assume no responsibility for your actions.

ISBN: 978-1-989840-08-5 (softcover)
ISBN: 978-1-989840-09-2 (hardcover)

Big Moose Publishing 08/2020

Dedication

For those who boldly embrace new ways of working that deeply align with who they are and who they are meant to be. And for my grandmother, the first and most influential entrepreneur in my life. Thank you for being courageous in your life so that I can be in mine.

CONTENTS

INTRODUCTION..1
   Why Real Girls Want Growth..................................1
   How Marketing Became a Problem.........................5
   Meet Your Real Girl Guide.......................................8

1: WHY AUTHENTICITY MATTERS......................................14
   Make Your Marketing Real....................................14
   Understand the Role of Marketing 17
   Follow a Real Approach...19
   Get Out of Your Way...20
   Confidence Isn't Key..21
   Take Small, Steady Steps..22
   Tap into Something Bigger....................................24

2: AUTHENTIC MARKETING...28
   Marketing Redefined..28
   Marketing as a Profound Act of Service...............29
   Traits of Authentic Marketing...............................36
      What Authentic Marketing Is Not...................36
      THOR: An Easy Acronym.............................41
      T Is for Transparent...42
      H Is for Honest...47
      O Is for Original 52
      R Is for Real 55
   What Gets In the Way of Authenticity?.................62
   The Need to Belong...64
   Other Reasons..67

3: BE YOUR WHOLE SELF..73
See Your Unique Design..73
Know Your Worth..84
It's Not Just You...85
Step Toward Your Purpose..91
Be Honest and Find Your Heart's Desire.....................96
Create Authentic Goals..98

4: FIND YOUR TRUTH...102
The Truth About Truth..102
What's True for You...105
What Is Too Much Truth?...110
When Your Truth Aligns With the Spiritual..............114
Your Why and How to Find It...................................118
What You Really Sell..125

5: CLEAR YOUR PATH FORWARD................................131
Lose the Contradiction..132
Use "Yes, and…" 135
Discover How Family Ties Can Bind.........................139
Play for Results and Move Ahead..............................145
Realize You're in the Right Place................................152
There's Nothing the Matter With You.......................152
Uncover Your Voice & Style.......................................157

6: AN AUTHENTIC MARKETING PLAN..........................166
Stop the Confusion..167
Make Your Plan...169
Admit Your Financial Goals......................................170
Study the Market...173
Find Your Resources..177
Ask the Right People..190
Celebrate Your Plan...193

CONCLUSION 196
  What's Next?..199

EXCERPT FROM THE NEXT BOOK
The Authentic Marketer Book Two: Love.........................203

ACKNOWLEDGEMENTS..211

INTRODUCTION

Why Real Girls Want Growth

The fullness of our humanity can be expressed only when we are true to ourselves. Your real job on earth is to become more of who you really are. Anything less is a faked life. – Oprah Winfrey

For me, this quote gets right at the point of life. Forget settling for nothing less than your best. We real girls won't settle for less than our true selves: the good, the bad, and the ugly. We don't want to be shallow, surface oriented, or just skimming through. We want to dive deeply and gulp from the well of a genuine life. This means we aren't necessarily concerned with the surface stuff of modern life. Don't get me wrong. It's not that we don't enjoy all the pleasure that can be had in this life. It's just that we don't think that's the whole enchilada. We may depend on our half caff, oat milk latte to get us fired up in the morning or that outfit on fleek to boost our confidence, but we never confuse that for the substance of a life that lets us express exactly who we are and what we are here to do. That's just how we dress it up.

We crave authenticity, not only in one area, but in all of them—in our relationships, our work, our families, our communities, and our time on the planet. We crave to express our real selves and have an authentic exchange with others. We yearn to dial into the rich, raw, and sometimes even raunchy bits of real exchange that make us feel something. We wish to feel truly alive and not just like we're passing time. Sometimes that means feeling the pain, sorrow, or grief that seems inevitable as life flows forward. Do we like the negative? Not necessarily. Are we insane? Nope. Just real. We just want all the trimmings that come with that package, even when they are less than ideal.

Growth is a constant in our world. Because real life keeps moving forward, we move with it. Life on planet earth is not a static thing. Look around you. There's a never ending flow of forward movement in nature and the cosmos. Not to say that there aren't seasons when things die back or lay fallow, but that happens only to get ready for the next season of growth. We girls are the same—we strive for growth as everything in nature does.

I am not talking about the rampant growth that seems to fuel modern society. The stance many big businesses take that growth, especially short term growth, means putting profits over the long term wellbeing of people/environment and should be pursued at all costs is just plain silly. We girls are not down with the old party line that shareholders' returns are all that matter. Instead, we want to pursue responsible growth, like we'd want in a healthy garden or forest. We want an ecosystem where things thrive in their own timing, at the right pace, urged forward by the elements and following the inner rhythms inherent in every system. When I use the word *rhythm* with my clients instead of words like striving or pushing ahead, they all sigh with relief. As busy women who

INTRODUCTION

want to have it all in a way that respects who we really are and all that we care about, the idea of a pace that is natural and not forced is something we can lean into.

I am talking about creating growth that lets us real girls, and all that we hold dear—be it our family, friends, business, community or whatever—be well supported. It's about having the opportunity to do what we came here to do, making our inner dreams come true, and being able to create the future we want to have, not just for our own benefit, but to benefit all the people we inevitably bring with us.

This brings us to work and money, which like it or not, is one of the levers that determines whether our lives are one of freedom and flexibility or of being stuck behind a desk missing out on personal time and what we love. Many of us have figured out how to create what we want in our personal lives. Our last frontier is figuring out the work life to go with it. It's not only about the money. It's also about getting to make our contribution. Each of us came here with something to offer. And for many, that offering extends beyond the bounds of our homes to serving others who could benefit and thrive from being served with our gifts and talents. So we dive into our own business as a way to hopefully bring this all together: authenticity, freedom, and contribution.

With this noble aim, we set off and are almost immediately confronted with this painful truth: to grow a business we have to grow ourselves. Being in business for yourself can be challenging. You face many decisions, a lot of responsibility, and tons of uncertainty. Up you fly one minute, on top of the world because it's working, then down you tumble the next, assaulted by doubt and wondering if you were cut out for this. It's similar to being on a roller coaster, but with no safety bar. It's the same in other areas of our lives such as parenting or relationships. These areas are deeply meaningful parts of our lives, and we want them to feel supportive, loving, and abundant. After all, aren't these the big goals in life that promise us unending happiness if we obtain them?

Herein lies the rub.

The very things that can bring you the deepest satisfaction and help you feel fulfilled in your life also bring about the most pain and potential for growth. Our true selves can be unveiled only when we drop the masks. We are complex beings with intellectual, emotional, physical, and spiritual components all blended together. If you can learn to show up for that dance with authenticity then you can begin to experience the richness the situation has for you. When you numb out, push against, deny, ignore, or distract yourself from experiencing what's in the situation, you are denying what's real for you.

The dance can be even more intense if you are one of the many sensitive or intuitive people in the world who consider themselves called to their business. Add in having any trauma, stress, or abuse in your lifetime, and the intensity heightens.

If you want to grow your business, you have to grow yourself

Never fear. In the chapters ahead, you will learn how to grow into more of yourself and, as a result, be more impactful in your business. As you become more aligned with yourself and who you really are, this will unfold naturally. Growth and accomplishment will happen with more ease and less stress.

Let's start your business growth journey with a look at your visibility and how to use it to make that real growth you crave in your business. Marketing is the place where the rubber of these hopes for your business and your personal life hits the proverbial pavement and starts to play out.

INTRODUCTION

How Marketing Became a Problem

Does marketing seem like a never-ending stream of hype to you? Or possibly that it's everywhere, all the time, pulling you away from things that matter like quality time with family or friends? Or that as a small business owner you must constantly be tending to and doing it? If so, you're not alone.

It wasn't always this way. Marketing has changed dramatically in the 21st century. Because of that, it's harder to get our heads around it, much less understand just how to use it to our advantage.

Why?

Because marketing in today's world organically flows rather than being a linear, logical thing. Marketing—the process a business takes to become visible to potential clients and to serve them—changes as often as services, products, and the people creating them do. This is why it can seem confusing at best, or at worst, overwhelming. Marketing fits into the broader context of the society it exists in. It's not static because, at a core level, it's about people and their commerce-oriented relationships that flow forward in the same never-ending tide that life does.

It didn't start this way.

Early on, marketing was defined more narrowly as the promotion and selling of products. That's because it literally came from the original source of commercial exchange: the actual market located in every town where merchants & farmers sold their goods. Even as the marketplace in each town was replaced by permanent stores, door-to-door, and other kinds of sales, the mindset remained that the market was for the products and goods that kept day-to-day life going. No wonder the early days of business—and marketing—were about promoting and selling goods.

At some point, business began to be about more than the

goods we need in our lives. As we crested the century change in the late 1800s, incomes crested with it, providing additional money for products beyond life's necessities. Meanwhile, the burgeoning industrial tide delivered more affordable, mass-produced goods.

Advertising blossomed to both bolster this trend and take advantage of it. The first billboard was created in 1900 for the waves of auto travelers who could now afford a car and a trip to the department store for conveniences for their homes. Advertising was the main method of marketing for nearly 50 years. Paying to put companies' names in front of consumers was all it took back then.

After a while, things began to even out. By 1950, products were so numerous and of such equal quality that paid announcements were no longer enough. That's when the idea of a soft sell came along, and products were tied to the emotional benefits people might enjoy when using the right product. Companies began inventing reasons why their product was different from another. You could gain sales by promoting the intangibles of your product such as safety, quality, and ease.

By the 1990s, big companies took this one step further and invented branding to distinguish nearly identical products from one another. Branding gave the company and its products a personality that a consumer could not only relate to, but also become loyal to. Now, companies don't just have products, they have an attitude, an approach, and a philosophy consumers can identify with. And with the advent of online sales, customers could buy anything they wanted and have it delivered to their door—with free returns if they didn't like it.

Branding was the answer to differentiating one company's "soft" benefits from another. It tapped into people's desires to be part of something. It tugged on the craving to be within

INTRODUCTION

a tribe where one feels seen, heard, and valued. It let people express themselves individually without fear of scorn or rejection.

Then came the Millennials. They actually want the soft differences to be a little harder, to be backed by something real. Companies like Patagonia, Zappos, and Toms, which exhibit authenticity in their voice and build their business around ideals that resonate with Millennials, have been richly rewarded. Consumers have responded eagerly to companies they feel good about buying from. Companies that embrace authenticity show solid growth.

We've come full circle. Marketing now needs to care for the actual market it's in as well as get a product or service noticed.

Authenticity in your marketing and business is the foundation for serving others

---

That's how we got to where we are today. As the title of this book implies, marketing today needs to be authentic. Getting visible in ways that feel right for your company and for your customers, being yourself and sticking to your ideals and genuine nature is what yields results. It also takes care of the people who provide your product or service and the people who use it. When it's done this way, marketing can be the foundation of service.

For small businesses, this encompasses a lot as our expanded definition of marketing begins in the early stages of penciling out the idea, and then continues with identifying the market that exists, and whether or not the idea continues to be marketable. It doesn't stop there. It carries on to developing the product or service in ways that fit what potential clients want. It flows, too, into customer service and encouraging repeat business—the bloodline for most businesses. Marketing then fosters the brand, or better put, the relationship between the company and its customers.

We have to marry all these logistical tasks with our human selves.

I'm here to reclaim authenticity in business for those of us who care. For us small business owners who want to be ourselves AND run a successful business that makes the world a better place. Who believe that being ourselves is truly a high calling. For those who see that the planet would be a better place if only we'd stop posturing or pretending and step into our fullness instead.

The practices and advice in this book will lead you toward and support you in feeling authentic in your marketing. We will address all aspects as a whole. If we only address your outer business marketing, you will be left feeling like a fraud on the inside. If we only address your inner self, you will push off your success until you feel better and your business will be neglected. The journey of stepping into your whole self gives you the whole package.

Finally.

Meet Your Girl Guide

Change comes slowly. Today, many so-called experts continue to teach old-school marketing methods—in spite of all the radical changes I just shared.

Anyone older than 30 likely grew up as I did hearing limiting ideas such as artists, teachers, or those who work with children can't make enough money to support themselves, you have to work hard for your money, money doesn't grow on trees, and nothing in life comes for free.

I was also warned to look out for anyone trying to con, swindle, or just plain ol' take advantage of me. I'm not sure

INTRODUCTION

why that was so important. Jokes about buying the Brooklyn Bridge or a piece of swampland in Florida were rampant even though where I lived in the Midwest, no one was actually swindled out of their life savings or anything else. Still, there was a definite distrust of sales, advertising, and anyone trying to "sell" you something.

In high school, I excelled at math and English but found them dry and slightly boring. The only thing that lit me up was art. That was when I found myself in my first bind. The only thing I liked to do supposedly wasn't going to support me financially. So instead, I enrolled as an engineering major in college when my father convinced me that being a woman engineer would open many financial doors. After a year of engineering classes I dropped it, because I could see there was simply no amount of money that could make my artistic nature mesh with people so dedicated to detailed calculations.

Instead, I chose graphic arts as my major and felt pleased that I had found a business way of working in art. But my very next thought was about the unsavory industry I was getting mixed up in. Advertising and marketing didn't fit with my mold of contributing any good to the world. Unfortunately, this line of thinking stayed with me throughout the first 18 years of my work life.

After college I moved to San Francisco, where the graphic arts were somewhat revered or at least, slightly cool. I found the flexible, creative nature of the work fit me well.

Success found me, and I ended up doing graphics for major companies like Jamba Juice, Disney, Kimpton Hotels & Restaurants, and Silicon Valley. I won awards for some clients and even got them big press coverage like in the Wall Street Journal and on the cover of WIRED magazine. But I still believed two things: that I couldn't make enough money being an artist and selling stuff to people was bad.

Along the way in my personal life, I tried to atone for my unsavory professional life. I followed a deep spiritual path to become the best person I could be. I delved into books by Louise Hay and worked through *The Artist's Way* by Julia Cameron. I participated in self-growth courses like the Hoffman Process and body-centered therapy groups. I became part of an ashram, learned how to meditate, and became a certified yoga teacher. I socialized with people determined to make our planet a better place to live.

Few in my professional life knew of my spiritual and personal growth orientation. I pretended my spiritual side didn't matter to my work. In my spiritual circles, I found it hard to admit I was in marketing. Instead, I opted to highlight my artistic nature. I was a graphic designer, not in branding; I was a freelancer, not an owner of a firm. In both worlds, I felt the need to downplay the other world so that I would be accepted.

To my credit, I did try to bridge the gap bit by bit. I moved towards the eco-side of the design business, using vendors who had green practices. Later, I let go of clients whose companies weren't making a positive impact, and I only worked for those who were making a contribution. But I still felt guilty.

In 2014, tired of the split and ready to finally do good with my work, I discovered coaching. I had enough mastery in the marketing world that I earned good money with only part-time hours each week, and I had time for school. I moved to a small rural area filled with like-minded folks and tried, once and for all, to quit this field and finally do something that made a difference. I wanted to become a life coach, to help others live bigger, fuller lives on their own terms.

In the process, I realized I could make a big difference right where I was. Rather than tossing out my 20+ years of marketing and branding experience, I could combine

INTRODUCTION

coaching and marketing to help entrepreneurs have bigger, fuller businesses on their terms. I had realized the truth that to grow your business, you need to grow yourself. And, for this, you need a coach. This allowed me to bring all my skills and gifts to impact others' lives in a significant way.

The biggest difference you can make is often right in front of you

---

Stepping into authenticity in my business has been the best career move I've ever made. I've grown my coaching business in these few years more than I ever did for the 18 years that I owned my design firm. I not only feel as though I'm in the right place, but also that I've found my calling. Every day I jump out of bed to do the work to move along my own business and my clients.

One more thing…

I want to share the way this book came about. In October of 2015, I didn't clear space on my calendar with the idea that it was time to write a book. Rather, I started to have an urge to write, which I couldn't ignore. When I sat down to write, the words that sprang to my mind weren't fully my own.

I don't know how to explain it other than to say that when I opened my mind to see what this urge to write had to say, all kinds of words came tumbling through, almost faster than I could type them. A little confused but curious, I allowed them to come. The amazing thing was how quickly and consistently they came. I could sit and write a thousand words in about 20 minutes with my eyes closed. My fingers seemed to have a life of their own.

Since I'd wanted to write a book for as long as I could remember, this felt pretty darn exciting. Books I had read about writing said to aim for a thousand words per day, and here I was banging that out in less than half an hour. I did this for about one month, and the book was born. Of course, that was only the beginning. It took the next four years to translate and organize these profound but densely packed messages so that they could be applied to my—or your—work lives.

Looking back, I would say this was the period of time when my professional and spiritual life finally came together. Sitting down to write while being in such flow, being inspired by concepts greater than my intellect could ever come up with alone, and tapping into what felt like a universal current felt as normal as breathing. I was no longer censoring myself to be logical and "normal" at work, but opening myself to take in information whatever way it came. This started happening in my workdays, too. In coaching, you are involved in really listening to another person to hear what's going on underneath what they are saying. I started to rely more on my intuition, gut instincts, and what I sensed as much as I did my intellect and knowledge. I even prayed for clients and their progress, for me to see things clearly and to serve in a bigger way.

It wasn't totally easy. Sometimes I questioned why this was happening to me and what it meant. Some days I longed to just go back to graphics and branding which seemed more straightforward. But if I was honest, that wasn't exactly true either. Looking back at the projects I had done, or awards we had won, there wasn't a clear black and white reason for any of it. What makes one marketing campaign or set of graphics work better than another? Where do those creative ideas come from anyway? We look back at successes in the marketing world and try to explain them logically, but in truth, there's always an element of mystery in every success. I see this even now with the entrepreneurs I work with. Yes, they learn new skills and take many actions to get their successful outcomes. But when we look back at exactly what it was, it can be difficult

INTRODUCTION

to name it precisely.

Marry the logical with the intuitive in your business for the best outcomes

---

I now look at it like a dance with the universe, or source, or God, or whatever you want to call it. We are part of a world that has some intangibles that cannot be explained exactly but can be interacted with. For best outcomes, we have to be in that dance as consciously as we can. When we are, miracles happen.

For me, bringing these two sides of myself together was a big part of me stepping into full authenticity. Now I routinely bring up normal, business type topics to my spiritual communities and spiritual concepts to my business community. I'm just as likely to do a little yoga when I'm at my desk, or to lead folks in a grounding exercise before we start a meeting. There's no longer a separation for me between work and spirituality. As such, my work life fulfills in ways it never did before. My own marketing has become easier, too, as I use many ways of knowing to guide my decisions. This lets the universe deliver all kinds of surprises to me, along with me building a steady set of skills to use on my own behalf.

Your journey will not necessarily be the same. You may have no need to merge your spirituality with your work. But perhaps you need to find your voice, or step into a larger version of your business and your dreams, or find all your real girl parts and invite them to the table. Whatever your needs, I hope this book helps you step into your full alignment.

1

WHY AUTHENTICITY MATTERS

Make Your Marketing Authentic

A uthenticity. An overused buzzword that has lost some of its original power. This happens often in our trendy culture when we sling about a concept in an attempt to corral behavior. When we research and refine a word to the nth degree so that we can tell companies how to profit from it and then promote that in the news, it soon becomes meaningless.

When I first wrote this book, I pushed against using this word for almost four years. I felt it was overused and timeworn. Instead, I told myself my mission was to help my readers become their whole selves. But isn't that authenticity? I realize now that it is.

I started hearing about authenticity in the early 2000s. The Millennials had come of age and were baffling traditional businesses. They didn't act like the consumers before them and big business was scrambling to understand what to do in response.

Studies were funded and news stories were rampant. I was 30 at the time, a definite Gen Xer and already living an artistically oriented life in San Francisco, so I only listened with one ear. I thought I was already embracing my authenticity and that it was about time businesses and mainstream folks started doing it, too.

Fast forward to 2016 when I'm writing a book on spiritual marketing. At least I *think* I am. The idea of authenticity keeps popping up, but I phrased it instead as "bringing your whole self" to your business. I thought the conversation needed to center on the spiritual. I saw it as the next wave or trend in business.

Although that's still true for me, I was missing a very important point.

In truth, if more people step into or embrace their spiritual nature in their work, they are not becoming "more spiritual". They are becoming more authentic. They are breaking down the walls of keeping their personal lives separate from their work. But only if that's authentic for them. For some, spirituality may have nothing to do with their authenticity.

As I continued to discuss spirituality as what we should embrace, I was denying the fact that we are all as unique as the universe itself. Not all are on the same path. Forcing spirituality upon all marketing efforts would be misguided. It's only a tool that some will use, and others won't.

Authenticity, or being your real self, can be seen as the pinnacle for any spiritual practice. Let yourself be fully *you* in your business, and you will be more successful. The path to finding and being our authentic selves is part of being human. We've been looking for ourselves throughout the ages. That's why in generations past, there have always been those who went against the grain and carved out their own path, even when it meant death or imprisonment. That's why each generation pushes against what was before them and tries to create a better way. That's why the personal growth industry commands 10 billion dollars per year.

Certainly being authentic counts as a fundamental value in the United States. We left the monarchy way back when because we wanted freedom. And, it wasn't any old freedom we were seeking. It was the freedom to live the way we wanted, worship the way we wanted, and pursue happiness as we saw fit. This fits with the Merriam Webster definition of authenticity which is "being true to one's own personality, spirit, or character."

This is not to leave out other parts of the world. For the most part, all cultures have fought to be free from control of others. We humans all seem to seek the right to live and rule ourselves as we like, including how we raise our children, partner up, and practice our spiritual yearnings. Wars have been fought for this right to be ourselves.

Authenticity, in addition to its definition of being true to one's own spirit or character, is further defined as "not false or imitation; real or actual."

When you are pretending to be something that you're not, or are conditioned to behave in a way not genuine to you, it takes a toll. It doesn't feel right; it feels dishonest and disturbs your peace. Think about any time you've had a big realization or aha and gotten really real with yourself about something. Didn't you feel amazingly peaceful after? Or when someone has shared something vulnerably honest about themselves, don't you feel closer to them? Being authentic gives life the very meaning you yearn for.

Authenticity creates the basis for a meaningful life

WHY AUTHENTICITY MATTERS

An ever present truth with the many entrepreneurs I work with boils down to this: if your business isn't where you want it to be, then things need to be done differently.

Often you want to start with something outside of you. If you could just find more hours in the day, master a new skill, or get that client to signup, then you could soar. Or going inward, you focus on what you believe you lack inside. If you could just be more confident or worthy, then you could finally have it all. But that just delays your success until you're "better". The journey of bringing out your whole self gives you the whole package.

Start by stepping inward, honoring who you are now along with who you can grow into being. Then, begin to authentically weave more of the inner you with the outer you. In the chapters ahead, I'll show you how. This book will help you find your right way forward.

Understand the Role of Marketing

Marketing can be a hot topic, partly because it comes with its own built-in hype. If you want to stay relevant, those in marketing tell you that you need to learn and follow an endless stream of best practices, new tips, tricks, and tools. Marketers are, after all, good at marketing.

Of course, it's not all hype. Marketing is crucial to a thriving business. Although selling and delivering the actual product or service may seem more critical to a business's survival, marketing acts as the gatekeeper that makes the sales possible. In reality, marketing weaves into nearly every aspect of a business. Marketing starts at the beginning with research to determine a market for a product or service. From there, it moves to the creation of the product itself, then on to how to price, promote, and distribute—including branding, packaging, and delivery—along with customer care and repeat business. Even warranty and returns are under the purview of marketing. Literally everything involved with any aspect of the business that touches the customer is driven by marketing.

Marketing also drives several intangibles like brand awareness, cause and community building, and environmental choices the company makes. Think of marketing as the support threads that everything else threads through in the fabric of your business.

> **Since marketing weaves among most aspects of your business, being authentic makes a large impact**

For entrepreneurs, especially purpose-driven ones, marketing can be uncomfortable. Our products and services are often personal. They flow from something we are passionate about and/or from our own hands. In some ways, we are our business, or at least the separation between our business and us seems thin. We are good at what we do and want to use our talents to make a difference to the world we are part of.

This means whatever difficulty we have in being our full selves shows up in our businesses. If we tend to focus on pleasing other people, that issue shows up in our pricing as we give too much for too little. If we have troubling finding our own voice, then we are likely to write generic marketing messages that don't impact potential clients or feel like we don't know what to say. If we are looking for other's approval, then we likely run from one effort in our marketing to the next, missing the success that results when we engage full heartedly from where we already are. Mostly when I see businesses that need help in their marketing, I see owners who need help stepping fully into their own power and holding a larger appreciation of themselves and their real capabilities. It's hard to create a successful business trying to be someone we're not.

For most of us, marketing differs from the business we are engaged in. Marketing and sales are skills we need to learn on top of the mastery of the product or service we offer. This can make authenticity problematic. While your craft may be well suited to your introverted state or your passion for detail, marketing asks for the opposite skill set. How can you be both? In addition, the massive information overload that generally surrounds learning marketing skills makes it really confusing.

Hyped language about "get rich quick" or "two simple steps," for example, doesn't lend itself to authenticity. We need to find language that works for us. As we learned how to do our marketing, who among us hasn't gone down paths that didn't pay off because they weren't a good fit for who we really are? We need genuine guidance.

Follow a Real Approach

I'm suggesting another way where you are true to your own character, real, and honest in your life. Now, bring that to your marketing.

This means doing marketing that actually fits you, not the marketing that you think you "should" be doing nor the latest shiny object or trend that makes you seem hip or in the know. Authentic marketing lets you be seen in all your brilliance, lets you be yourself, and makes you visible to enough people to make the impact you want to make.

Good marketing comes from your state of mind. It's not a long to-do list, never-ending campaigns, or endless copywriting and social media. It's an all-embracing approach to achieve visibility for you and your business. Simply stated, marketing is a willingness to be seen by and connect with other people. Your mind and body state have everything to do with that.

**Good marketing comes from who you are being,
not what you are doing**

Instead of hunching over a computer looking for ways to market yourself, stretch yourself. Head out of the house to meet people and discover what life brings your way. Marketing thrives on a positive attitude and openness to life.

Get Out of Your Way

You may be thinking, "What about those online marketing people who earn seven figures all from their laptop? I want to do that!" Here's a little secret—most seven-figure business people are highly visible in their industry and are often out speaking at conferences and meeting people who can move their businesses forward. A tiny sliver of folks (in the .001%) may truly live in their cave of isolation and make money, but odds are, it won't be either you or me.

If you think you can't get clients or work done by being out in the world, please reconsider. One of my favorite clients, Nancy, caught my attention at a newly formed women's business meeting I attended as a favor to its organizer. There were only seven of us there, and we listened to a speaker for most of the meeting. However, Nancy's one-minute introduction at the beginning of the meeting stood out to me so much that after the meeting, I asked her to tell me more about her story. She was struck by my quick understanding of her background and how that connected to the work she was doing now. She hired me one week later to help tell her story in an important proposal. Four years later, she's not only a valued client, but a friend and colleague. Another of my clients came to me because I made a nice connection with his wife in the park while pushing our daughters on the swing.

My clients routinely find that when they step forward with who they are and what they want, things begin to unfold with more ease. They get asked to speak on their topic, new opportunities arise, and they get clients.

If you stay isolated, it's like the universe, source, God, or whatever you happen to call it, wants to send you answers to what you are asking for but can't get through. You must get out and be open to receiving.

Confidence Isn't Key

Of course, you won't make the right connections if you aren't your full genuine self. If you are only showing the world part of yourself, you'll only get met partway. Others can sense when you are disconnected from part of yourself or aren't comfortable with all of what makes you the real you. I'm not talking about confidence either. Although widely promoted as being the key to making your business rock, it's not. Being real is.

This explains why even beginners can make progress in their business and get clients. If you are honest about where you are and what you offer, and are deeply connected with all of yourself, you have all you need to move your business along, even if you aren't exactly sure just how.

Confidence comes after doing something for a while. Sure, that makes your business feel easier, but it goes away again as soon as you bring in a new effort or direction in your business. This happens all the time as a business grows. In other words, confidence cycles in and out of your business based on the newness of the effort. Successful people often say that they have no idea if the next thing will work or not. Don't use confidence as the marker for whether to move forward or not. Admit you're not sure and carry on.

That's an authentic approach: being real about what is.

Nope, we don't know if this next thing will work. Nope, we aren't exactly sure who makes the best client for the type of work we're doing. Nope, we aren't exactly clear on our next steps. But we are here, and bringing as much of ourselves along as we can, and that is the best we can do. Luckily, it's enough.

Take Small, Steady Steps

This book will help you step into your authenticity around marketing. Although the end may feel worth it, your journey won't be all sunshine and roses. This book may challenge the way you think and present ideas you find difficult to implement or hard to sustain.

Living as your true self is simple. I said simple, not easy

Well, welcome to life. What things are worth doing that don't challenge us, at least at first? Once you accept the challenge, you are on your way to a life within your business that you've only dreamed of. You'll even find the universe will meet you partway, sending you support in the form of people, ideas, and opportunities you could never imagine from where you're standing now. So get to it. You'll never reach the endpoint if you don't take your first steps.

This book will show you how to explore and discover your own path. I will share steps that have worked for me and my clients to encourage and inspire your forward movement. All you have to do is you start where you are.

I can help you make shifts from where you are to where you need to be. Like when you focus on what you are giving people–the tools or the means that your products or services offer—rather than on where they can go if they employ the tools you give them. Every day I look at copy or marketing materials from earnest entrepreneurs who want very much to help other people. And all their messages are about the "what" of their business. What they are giving in their program, or what they are going to do when clients arrive in their office, or what clients can expect from them and their team in working together. It's all surface oriented to the physical or experiential of their work. People don't buy the what. They buy the result that they want.

People buy the outcomes they want to have

Your marketing materials have to show people the results they can enjoy if they use your product or your service. You have to show how your "what" can solve their problem or meet their dream. Even if you sell something simple like a kitchen utensil, they are buying it to make their life easier, to get a better result in their cooking, or to meet their dream of being a great cook or homemaker. You have to market to those desires if you want a thriving business. Many entrepreneurs I see need to learn to message their service or product from this new perspective.

A shift like this in your messaging requires that you take many small steps. You have to take in the information that you need to be doing it differently, learn new skills to do it, try variations until it's effective, and catch yourself when you're slipping back into your old habits. Any one of these efforts may have multiple steps to enact it. To make lasting change that gets you better results, you have to commit to taking many small, steady steps to get there. There is a lot of information like this in this book (and, more in book two and three on this same subject). All the steps are practical and doable, but each ask you to step into different.

To get the most out of the book, I suggest you quiet your mind and experience the material, rather than analyzing it as you read. I often recommend the same for my clients in all their marketing endeavors. Let's start this practice now. In this way, the ideas in the following pages can begin to work with you in the way they are meant to—authentically.

Tap Into Something Bigger

You might ask how to quiet your mind when you're reading new and empowering ideas. At first it can be challenging—everything feels exciting and you want to get started right away—but you'll likely get even more out of the experience if you shift—and open—your consciousness beyond just your own energy. Instead of jumping to conclusions (new ideas are stimulating so it's easy to get carried away), take a deep breath and sit with them for a while.

For some, meditation may be their path, but that's not the only way to stop the chatter and go deeper within. Take a breath. Sit quietly. Tune into nature. These can all help you connect with the subtle flow of consciousness around you. When you do this, you are changing the state of your brain waves, working on all the cells in your body. As you practice this, you will begin to feel how profoundly life-affirming it can feel. When you tune into this larger flow of energy, you are channeling divine inspiration that seeks to find a connection in the world. Not surprisingly, this is exactly what you are trying to do with your marketing.

You may already be familiar with this state of flow. Many of you do this when you get really into something and lose track of time, or say you don't know where that idea came from. As children, we used to do this more naturally, more frequently, before we grew up and experienced the push on productivity.

WHY AUTHENTICITY MATTERS

Mulling something over or giving it time to gestate used to be common ways of dealing with issues or problems. But the ego (and our driven culture) stepped in and demanded you to willfully react to things rather than hand them over to the larger consciousness you are part of. I encourage you to start your work by shifting from the small you to being part of the larger flow.

The following exercise can support you in accessing this flow in your marketing. You may want to record yourself reading it aloud so that you can relax into it. Or if you want to download this meditation as an audio file, go to lindabasso.com/authenticmarketer.

Sit comfortably with your eyes closed. Breathe naturally for several breaths, not forcing your breath to do anything different from what it may be doing. Now, imagine your breath coming in from one side of yourself and going out the other. You might imagine the air currents coming toward you from the right, going into your right nostril, circulating through your body and then, out your left nostril to join the air currents on the left side of your body. Stay with this breathing for several minutes.

Now, extend this imagining farther out and see that the air currents coming from your right are actually connected to many things in the world: the objects that it passes over, the other people and animals that it breathes through. You can see this connection as millions of tiny golden threads that weave around and through everything, coming into and through you too. As you breathe out to the left, you send the golden threads on their journey to connect with the world around you. You are part of everything you are surrounded by. You have a place in it, and so does everything else. Sit in this golden web, breathing for several more minutes.

When you do an exercise like this, you are signaling something important and concrete to your mind and body: that you are part of a vast web of interconnection in this world. This prepares you to start noticing the connective energy always flowing toward you so that you can pull from the larger energy moving through our world. If you are tempted to dismiss this as too simple, please don't. Professional athletes, famous actors, high-performing leaders, and executives all use visualization to accomplish exactly what they create in their mind's eye. Science allows us to see that our body can't distinguish the difference between something really happening around us or vividly imagined. The body releases the same hormonal and physical shifts in either case. If you want to be tuned into the connections around you, use this powerful tool of visualizing it to bring it to being.

As we'll explore throughout this book, there are many ways to be authentically inspired. Maybe you already see how much you'd benefit from this path. In today's business world, it's clear not all people do. Many spend their weekends seeking a more authentic stance with their yoga classes and self-help books, only to arrive Monday morning in their business to force things ahead, no matter the cost.

Practice tuning into the flow around you in small ways and it will become easier in the big things

---

It's not the amount of activity or time that you spend being authentic at work that counts. It's the overall frame of mind and ongoing cultivation that you do. You could spend an entire day in your garden, but if you left it alone for the rest of the month, that day would be lost in weeds. Instead, tend to your garden, day by day. A little bit of weeding done every day never lets the overgrowth begin in the first place.

WHY AUTHENTICITY MATTERS

The same goes with work. Your one-day retreat, although growthful, may not do much for the rest of your work month. A few small actions taken toward authenticity every day can sustain you for the rest of your career. Don't be fooled by the smallness of the actions you can take. As Mother Teresa said, "Not all of us can do great things. But we can all do small things with great love."

2

AUTHENTIC MARKETING

Marketing Redefined

Earlier, I mentioned that at its most basic, marketing is about being visible to others. It's also about increasing your ability to serve and accurately inform people so that they can make good choices. For a larger company, that's a neutral process. After all, it's not about any one person.

But in a small business, it's all about you. That's a lot of pressure. Add in how visible you're becoming through all the connections you're making, and you can begin to feel vulnerable. This is especially true if you have stress, trauma, or abuse in your background when you likely learned being visible or connecting to others wasn't always safe. This makes authenticity such an important concept.

Think about it. If you can't be yourself in the business that's just you, how could you ever feel good in your business?

You can't accurately inform others about what your business does if you don't know yourself how you are different from others who offer a similar product or service. Not to mention, it takes a lot of energy to pretend to be something that you're not. Your strengths come from being your full self. You are best suited to serve others when you are bringing all of you to your work.

As much as we wish it were, marketing is NOT a one-size-fits-all proposition. The marketing that brings you success will be radically different from the kind that brings your colleagues and competitors success. That's why it can be totally crazy-making to find the right fit. But it's also a blessing. Because authentic marketing is not a one-size-fits-all proposition, you can find the bits and parts that work for you and leave the rest. I'm here to give you permission to do your marketing in *your* way— to find your authentic voice and approach and to carve out your own path that feels good.

Marketing As a Profound Act of Service

Are you a purpose-driven entrepreneur? Do you believe your product or service somehow contributes to the greater good of others or the planet?

As a marketing coach, I work with small business owners like you. They are not all environmentalists or healers, though some are. They often run regular types of businesses like hair salons, dance studios, or bookkeeping firms. What do they all have in common? They share a deep desire to express themselves authentically and from a sense of purpose. They sense that they've been called to their work or see that by doing their work, they are making a unique contribution to their clients. They often admit that many others are probably offering their service in ways that may sound better or more profitable, but they hold that knowledge alongside the belief that they are offering what they can, in a way that feels unique to them.

Good marketing increases your ability to serve others and make the world better

---

They believe the work they are doing makes the world better, too. They make it better in both small ways, like making their clients' days easier or helping their clients accomplish something, and in big ways, when they help their client meet a lifelong goal, impact the environment in better ways, or be of service to thousands of others. Often, when questioned about this, they flash a sheepish grin and get a "Pinch me, I can't believe this is real" look on their faces.

Usually, they have arrived at this stage in their business with what they believe to be little or no marketing. It's all been word of mouth or one thing leading to another. They often believe they don't have much in the way of marketing skills and come to me because they need to do "real marketing" in order to keep their business going or growing. Other times they have some marketing savvy, but haven't really enjoyed it, either because the system they've followed doesn't feel authentic to them or because they feel that doing the marketing keeps them from their "real work."

Growth is a constant in their world. Just as they reach one stage in life, other stages begin to unfold. The words "it's always something" are spoken often in their business circles or at dinner with friends. This rings true in their personal life, their business, or both. Often they are personally growing at a rapid rate to keep up with all this change. They flip between being exhilarated and exhausted. It's no wonder they question what they're doing, right and wrong.

I, too, am one of these purpose-driven entrepreneurs. As

I grow both my business and myself, I continue to step into emerging spaces. With each step, I'm asked to become more of the person I am and leave all my doubts and small-self parts behind. Along the way, as I garnered the courage to try new things, I discovered a powerful truth: marketing doesn't get in the way of my real work; instead, it's an act of service.

Marketing, when done well, is a profound act of service

I've been using this phrase when I give talks to groups of small business owners. And when I say it, the room gets a little quieter. There's a moment of reflection as the possible importance of this phrase sinks in. People who came to figure out their marketing—what they're doing right, what they're doing wrong, what could be better—take a breath. They heave a tiny sigh of relief.

Why?

Because it touches on the deeper level of why they are trying to figure out their marketing in the first place. Every solopreneur and small business owner I know wants to figure out their marketing so that they can make a greater contribution.

They've been thinking of marketing as a necessary evil to be done first *before* they can make their contribution. They are relieved by the good news that their marketing—which takes up a lot of their time—can be part of the contribution.

Why is marketing an act of service? Think about how much information comes at any one of us every single day. Most lack the time and concentration to sort through it all and understand what fits and what doesn't. Instead we end up feeling barraged and overwhelmed.

When you are genuine in your marketing and present

your services/products for what they can truly do for another person in a way that allows them see that this fits—or does not fit—then you are doing them a huge favor. Helping them to cut through the clutter and make good decisions certainly counts an act of service.

Think about that next time you are dragging your feet on creating your messaging or campaign. Would you approach it differently if you considered it an act of service instead of another item on your to-do list?

Your marketing also serves you and your business. If you don't earn enough money, you can't keep being of service to others. Sadly, this happens for many businesses. Others end up not making it off the ground as they start their small business while still earning money in another way. The workload becomes too much and they give up. I don't want to see either of these happening to you!

What happens when you don't feel authentic in your marketing? Typically one (or all!) of these happen:

1. You don't do it.
2. You only do it minimally.
3. You do it ineffectively.

Those in the first group dream of growing their business, or want to start something new within their existing business, but are long on talk and short on action. Phrases like "I know I should be..." or "One day when I have time I'll..." often come up in conversation. Typically they know that they don't love marketing or don't like doing certain parts of it, but they don't connect that with their failure to act. Instead of identifying what they don't like, or what isn't in alignment with them, and working to resolve the dilemma (or find another way of doing it), they are paralyzed by this misalignment. By just not doing their marketing they avoid the uncomfortable feelings of doing an activity that doesn't fit—but ultimately fail.

The second group feels familiar to me. I spent 18 years running a business that I wasn't aligned with. As a result, I did only the bare minimum to market it. I let it coast along bringing in just enough business to fuel my life but not enough to feel like I had a thriving, fulfilling business. It was a weird place as I was half in, half out all of the time. I describe it as surviving, not thriving. If this feels familiar to you, then you know it's a hard way to live. Only doing something to the bare minimum is a clear signal to yourself that there is something that lacks alignment that you need to address. Not doing anything about it disregards your own needs. This eats away at your self-esteem and creates a vicious cycle.

The third group fits many of the entrepreneurs I see out and about. They are taking massive action but not getting the results they hope for. This feels confusing and frustrating. They begin to feel "It must just be me" or "I'm doing something wrong."

Not so!

Usually they are not in alignment in their marketing or business and even though they are taking the "right" action, the flow doesn't happen because there's a kink in the pipe.

> *Jackie is in the home birth industry and has a full practice helping new mothers with their newborns. Her interest isn't just in helping her clients. She also feels a deep longing to contribute to her industry and to make a difference for other birth workers. So she spent part of her time in a birth worker collective and teaching for a nationwide birth education company. Although she loved doing the actual work with either group, she felt somewhat at odds with whether it was the right fit for her. Marketing either effort was a strain. She often felt frustrated when putting together her marketing materials or doing outreach for either group. Since she felt torn by using her time in this way and being with her own*

family, she did the bare minimum of what she needed to do. And worse, her efforts weren't bringing in clients for her classes or the collective. Clearly something needed to change.

As Jackie began to explore letting these groups go, a new longing emerged. She realized that her real alignment lay not in these particular two groups but in contributing in a meaningful way to her overall industry. She had an idea to create an event that brought together people in her industry to have meaningful conversations and create more harmony among the different groups within it. She began to create this event and although it was a lot of work to bring it about, the flow was undeniable. Where previously in the collective, she was shy to be a spokesperson at an event, she now held the role of the host for her own event with relative ease. Where previously she felt frustrated doing outreach to gather clients for her classes, now she boldly stepped into making her event highly visible and even reached out to gain sponsors for it.

Yes, she still felt the strain of needing to split her time between her work and her family but she did it with the belief that both were valid and contributed to her having a meaningful life. It became more of a balancing act and less of a tug of war. With everything flowing more easily, Jackie was able to market her event well and it was successful. She now has several more scheduled. Yes, she still has the same 24 hours to get things done but from a place of alignment it all happens with more ease and the results make it worth it.

Clearly, not feeling authentic in your marketing can hurt your business. On the other hand, amazing things are in store when you work toward being genuine in your marketing. Here are a few:

1. **You create more value:** You are happy to become visible to the people you can serve, who are literally waiting

for the product or service that you offer, and you are making a valuable difference in their lives. This means loving the people you serve so much that you want to know what they struggle with, what their dreams are, and what they need in order to move forward in their lives. Then you respond by creating products and services that solve those problems or help them live into those dreams. They, in turn, are able to contribute more to the world around them, as they become more capable, whole people. This creates the win-win-win of authenticity. It adds value to your life, to your clients, and to the world.

2. **You're more profitable:** People can sense your alignment when you are authentic in your marketing. It makes it easy to know, like, and trust you, which leads to you getting hired. If you've had the opposite experience with someone, you know exactly what I mean. When you feel someone is not genuine, you want to get away from them and whatever they are selling. They feel pushy and fake. But when you are with that genuine, aligned person, you consider what they are selling with more ease. Also, when you feel authentic in what you are selling, you are willing to do more of it. That's certainly the way to higher sales!

3. **You have more enjoyable days:** Feeling out of alignment or like you're not being true to yourself doesn't feel good. Fatigue, dread, doubt, and inactivity are your constant companions. In contrast, being authentic in your business creates a wonderful flow. You feel curious, excited, and at ease about your efforts. Sure, maybe you don't love every single moment, but you're even authentic about that, which allows you to do the mundane tasks that every business requires knowing that they, too, are part of the picture and afford you the opportunity to do the parts that you love. Your days are filled with this win-win-win thinking, and you often feel fulfilled and happy with what you accomplish.

Traits of Authentic Marketing

Understanding why marketing matters and how it can serve us forms only part of the picture. We need to explore the edges, texture, and shape of what defines authenticity in marketing. Here we'll dive into the characteristics of authentic marketing in more detail. We'll look at what it's not, what it is, and what may stand in your way of achieving it.

What authentic marketing is not

Why start with what authentic marketing is not? Many misconceptions surround authenticity. Part of that comes from the tension discussed earlier. We may have been born into a group that doesn't focus much on being authentic. Perhaps while growing up, after our family moved to a new city or state, or other childhood circumstances, we found ourselves feeling quite different from the people around us. To satisfy our need to belong, we squelched parts of ourselves in order to better fit in. Or maybe it's the nature of being human, that those things we long for don't always come easily and naturally but rather are formed from the grit of experience. Similar to a pearl, our authenticity may come in response to both the negative and positive experiences we have around it. Let's break down a couple of these misconceptions.

First, authenticity is not always comfortable. In fact, it can actually feel downright unfamiliar and awkward. For example, many of us went into business for ourselves after another job or business stopped feeling like a good fit. We stepped into our current business because it was a more authentic expression of our gifts, talents, and the contribution we want to make in the world.

How comfortable was that transition? I often felt as though I were groping around in the dark, not able to see what was next and not at all sure why I had stepped into this unfamiliar place. Was it also exciting? Yes. But I questioned myself over and over in the first few years as I learned many new skills and stepped through unfamiliar territory. This can happen every time something new emerges in our business or personal life.

Your measure of authenticity should not be whether it feels comfortable. It likely won't. Too often I see people stop their pursuit of their authenticity because of this misconception. When they think that being more authentic will only feel good, it creates confusion and frustration because of unrealistic expectations.

It makes sense, right? Naturally we feel out of our comfort zone when we step into new skills or emergent spaces. That has nothing to do with being your authentic self. Instead you are having the natural experience of being a beginner at something. If you've ever watched a child learning something new, you can see how messy, imperfect, and full of falling downs it is.

As adults, however, we've gotten used to a certain amount of comfort. Anticipating the discomfort, or even the perceived discomfort, that accompanies any change can often be enough for us to avoid our authentic desires in favor of the status quo.

Having lived through this cycle many, many times in my own pursuit of authenticity, I can honestly say that, in the end, your authenticity will come to feel more comfortable than living in an inauthentic situation. Sure, you may experience some uncomfortable steps along the way, but it's worth it.

Let's say you realize that some of your clients aren't really in alignment with you. Maybe they want more than they are paying for, they don't have a sense of humor, or they don't step forward on their own but rather keep letting you fix what's broken in their world. You may have to hold back a part of yourself in order to make it work with these clients.

Heading toward being your whole self in your business will ultimately make you more comfortable. Getting there will mean having uncomfortable moments, as you get honest about what you've been disregarding in yourself. You may have conversations or policy changes that move these clients into different behavior or out of your business. You may have to deal with and manage fears about whether this will all work out in your favor. Is this process authentic? Yes. Comfortable? Not necessarily.

Authenticity is not always spontaneous or carefree. Movies often portray authenticity as something we just "know" about ourselves and feel compelled to follow. One day the main character wakes up and knows it's time to do something differently. Or after a series of difficult situations, they realize who they really are and suddenly take a new path.

Not so in real life.

Much of finding and being our authentic selves comes from deliberate thinking and reflection, including the long, slow process of journaling, therapy, and observing what is rather than what we wished were true. It's like an archeological dig where we must delicately and slowly unearth many fragments of ourselves from the dirt, sometimes finding only the tiniest shards, carefully brushing them off and examining them in context of all the other fragments we are finding in order to understand what we've discovered.

Good news! Deliberate thought doesn't make you less authentic. In fact, slowing things down and letting the situation emerge is one of my favorite ways of finding my authentic answer. When my discoveries come about in this way, what gets uncovered tends to be the real thing. Along these same lines, this journey isn't totally carefree. Often our authentic desires ask us to make change, negotiate new roles, and step toward unfamiliar places. Because most of us are part of groups like family systems, businesses, and communities, this often means we have to take care of others in our journey toward finding ourselves. This can usually be done in a way that preserves the relationship, but it often requires a thoughtful, careful approach to maintain our ties and while making the needed change.

The same principle applies to commitments and finances. Suddenly pulling out of our commitments or putting ourselves into financial difficulties may not be the easiest path toward authenticity. In fact, unlike the Hollywood version where the lead character dumps their life in favor of a new one, moving too fast toward authenticity can make it much harder to get there at all. Instead of heading toward the ease of ourselves, we end up dealing with the chaos of survival.

Instead, embrace the idea that a deliberate, considerate approach can serve not only you but also all that you care about. Making a plan to launch a new part of your business while you earn money from your existing clients might get you to your authentic job more quickly than letting go of your financial stability and trying to sink or swim.

Authenticity is not about letting it all hang out. There are many flavors to this misconception from the idea that being authentic means being brutally honest, to doing whatever you want to when you want to, to saying whatever comes to mind. However, being authentically you never calls for being rude, inconsiderate, or inappropriate. Even if it seems authentic for you to yawn and roll your eyes when that one colleague starts in on her same story for the 100th time, that's not the answer. Authenticity would have you look at what's real for you and make a conscious decision, not act out like a teenager. If you are willing to bear the consequences of making a change in the relationship and really need to because that moment of boredom is authentically more than you can bear, then a direct conversation has to be had, or you must find a new behavior to shift the situation toward something more bearable. Maybe you have to stop attending these meetings or shift teams for example.

If you are feeling uneasy or less than confident in a situation, it's OK to share that with people who are in your support system like a good friend, colleague, or spouse, so that you can get it off your chest and decide how/what needs to be done to get you to confidently do it. But it's not correct to share those fears with the client who just hired you. If someone asks for your opinion on their project and you think it stinks, you don't get to say that, because in truth, even if your final judgment seems to be that the project won't work, don't label the why as "it stinks." Instead be sure that in your professional experience aspects of it aren't correctly setup. Then you can share in a tactful way what's authentic to you. If it's authentic to you that you'd rather not comment, you get to say that. In a sense, you do get to do what you want, but you need to do it consciously, not reactively. It needs to be professional and courteous. And you need to know that there will be consequences that you have to weigh beforehand and decide if they are worth bearing. Your actions will bring up other's genuine reactions. There's no free pass on consequences because you were being "authentic."

Authenticity is not always unique to you. In my years of meeting with many different people, I have seen so many variations in each of us that it's mind-boggling. Truly we are all designed uniquely. Having said that, some things unite us as humans and we share a tremendous amount of similarity. We have some universal behaviors. For instance, all humans make the same facial expressions for core emotions like happiness, surprise, and anger. This is innate and global, found in every culture across our planet. Even a blind child will make the facial expression despite having never seen another person do it. This suggests that we have some common core emotions. We all seem to seek love and connection with others and will do so across kinship lines for groups with shared values like religions, sports, tribes, teams, and politics. Music has been a part of every human grouping. Caregivers and infants form socio-culture connections in every culture. We all laugh. These shared traits often mean that what we value or find to be in our authentic nature contain similarities to many other people. Don't get hung up on how similar or different you are to others. Yes, be sure that you are discerning what's authentic for you rather than blindly following trends or being unduly influenced by others. But don't worry if your authentic nature has similarity with someone else's as it doesn't diminish yours in any way.

Having explored what authentic marketing is not, let's look at what it is.

THOR: An Easy Acronym

I always write by brainstorm first, letting my thoughts and ideas just pour onto the page. Then I go back and do any necessary research or reworking to make ideas flow. When I looked over what I had written on the traits of authentic marketing, I was struck by the beginning letters of my four traits of authentic marketing. They seemed to form a word. Hort? Roth? Ah, yes, maybe Thor. I wondered if the Norse God could offer any insight on our authenticity conversation or if it was merely a funny little coincidence.

It turns out that Thor was the god of the sky and protector of humans. He ruled fertility, family, agriculture, and weather. Humans called on him to solve problems, bless their unions & ventures, and ensure that food and weather both supported them. Basically, Thor provided everything needed to support human life! Authenticity acts in the same way—it's everything you need to have a good human experience. And THOR just makes it easy to remember the four traits.

THOR: T Is for Transparent

If there is one quality in the authenticity conversation that scares people, it's this one. Our culture places a high value on looking like you have it all figured out. In contrast, being transparent can leave us feeling exposed and vulnerable. If we let ourselves and our decisions be seen, we wonder if there will be some pushback. We are afraid of being judged for our decisions.

Like it or not, authentic marketing needs to be transparent.

Consumers today are not as interested in the pretty, scripted versions of your company. They want to know who's really running it, how things are done, how money is spent, and even profit margins. They want to be sure they trust and respect your company before doing business with you. It's a little bit like an investor doing research before investing in a company. Customers know they have a choice in where they spend or "invest" their money. They will often choose to buy from one company over another based on transparency—or the lack of it.

I use the word "invest" because on the energetic level, anytime we exchange energy such as time or money with another, we are investing a part of ourselves. You would do well to ask for transparency from your clients as well. It would not serve you to have customers who don't fit your brand's values buying and using your products/services. Imagine if you sold healthy pet food with a mission to foster the health and well being of animals and found out that someone was using your pet food laced with poison to kill unwanted puppies. This would be a terrible fit for your company. The same goes for giving your services to people who are doing destructive things in the world. We all have the responsibility to build the planet we want to live in; transparency can be a real step towards doing that.

I like to think about this concept of transparency like a window into your business. As a person, you are out in the world and can be seen living life: going to the grocery store, hanging out with friends and family, and talking about what matters to you. Professionally, you are working with vendors, serving clients, and existing within a community of other businesses. In other words, because you exist in the world and interact with others, you are being seen by them.

This discussion centers on whether your window is clear or frosted, and if frosted, by how much. Being transparent means being your real self in all these settings, not acting like you think you are "supposed" to.

I had a client tell me recently that she tried to maintain a very professional, dialed back tone when she talked with and emailed her clients and editors. Yet in real life she's warm and conversational so in her work emails and calls she did not sound at all like her real self. She was doing this because she was trying to be like an image she had in her head of how someone who was "really" successful would act. This caused her work to feel very pressured as she tried to figure out just the right things to write and say. In fact, whenever she sat down to write something to share about her company, she froze wondering if it would come out right.

This happens more often than you think. I routinely see small business owners who feel like they don't know what to say, don't know if their actions are "right", and would never dream of sharing their inner thoughts and feelings with their colleagues and clients. Yet, this is the very thing that others crave from us. When you can be yourself, others feel more relaxed and at ease with you. They feel that you are reliable because they can tell you aren't hiding anything. In a world where trust causes someone to do business with us, or not, transparency is the fastest path to having enough clients.

You may be wondering the appropriate amount of transparency. What's too much? What about too little? What things should you be transparent about and are there any that are just TMI? Conversely, are you wondering why on earth anyone would care to know anything personal about you? Does that make you feel vulnerable? The answers lie in the literal definition of seeing through something. It ranges from being fully clear like clear glass, or frosted like a bathroom window that lets in light but softens the full picture. How do you decide on the amount transparency?

For many younger people, this step does not present a problem. Raised in an era of transparency in social media, they have no problem with the idea that transparency and privacy can coexist. In fact, they may have to consider the opposite issue: when is transparency too much for the other person or the situation at hand?

But if you are Gen X or older, this can be a process you need to work through. We were raised in an era where businesses definitely were not transparent. Transparency was not encouraged in school or the workplace. We were told to be professional at work and keep our personal lives to ourselves. It was only after the rise of the internet and how quickly information could be shared that transparency became a topic of conversation around politics and education in the mid 1990s. The topic of transparency in business came after the shift to the new millennium. If you weren't an active part of this conversation, you might still have questions about how much to share and when the time is right to share.

Whether you are grappling with too much or too little, the answer comes together with another concept: what's appropriate content? According to Webster, appropriate means especially suitable or compatible. While suitable conjures up an image of a stuffy formal dinner to me, the word compatible stirs my heart. It means *capable of existing together in harmony.* That's a definition I can get behind. Like the question of whether our window is clear or frosted, it depends on where it's needed.

As I mentioned, it used to be inappropriate to be transparent at work, but now that's changed. However, being too transparent in the wrong circumstance can disturb harmony. It's not about wearing different masks for different situations. It's about discernment. We went through a period of radical honesty, but that didn't work. It came about because people were ready to throw off the shackles of dishonesty and abuse of power, but it was over the top. It's about degrees of sharing and timing. It's also about being human.

By now you can see there's no black and white answer. It's a combination of where you are sharing, what company or brand values you have, and who you are sharing it with.

In action, it means not hiding things under the guise of privacy or internal systems in your business. Transparency calls for letting customers see the various aspects of your business: from how you source products, to your values, to decisions you make, to how your pricing works and how money is spent within your business. It means sharing your process in terms of both what has worked and what has not.

Get it right and you end up with customers who are loyal to you and your brand.

Take a look at these two things to determine how transparent you should be:

- **Your ideal clients and their desire for transparency:** Ideally, you are transparent in a way that matches the expectations of your ideal clients. After all, we are talking about your marketing, which means how transparent you are in being visible to others. The others you want to consider should be your ideal clients, not your family, friends, or well-meaning colleagues. If your ideal clients expect to hear a lot about what you think or do in your personal time, then you need to share that. Ditto if they expect you to keep that to yourself. For example, if your ideal clients are Millennials, they will expect a higher level of transparency than if your clients are Gen X or older. If your clients need to trust you with their private affairs such as money, intellectual property, or intimate affairs then they may not want to see you exhibiting a high level of transparency, while clients who rely on you to bring out their own vulnerabilities may expect you to be sharing intimate details of your own life. Take time to consider your ideal clients and what they'd like to see. If you're not sure, you may need to start asking them.

• **The level of transparency in your industry:** You also have to consider what the levels of transparency are in your industry. In the financial industry, for example, it's expected that information is kept private. Ditto for technology and law. Coaching, on the other hand, is more open with coaches routinely sharing how they move through their lives, sharing their personal experiences and decisions. Look around your industry to see how much or how little people typically share. There's likely to be a bit of a range here and your goal is to find a style and amount that feels like a fit for you.

When you blend your industry and clients, you get the right amount of transparency for your marketing. Let's say you are in the financial industry, which tends to have less transparency in it. How your company does its work may not be typically be shared. Let's say your ideal clients are Millennials. Then you would do well to be seen as a rule breaker and bringing more transparency to how your company does the financial work, like sharing fee amounts, or how you share profits, and causes you support, as these younger clients will feel more loyalty and connection with a company that shares in this way. Even though it pushes you toward an edge in your industry, it pushes you closer to your clients. Conversely, if you are a coach, but for older clients or clients who've experienced trauma, you might want to be seen as slightly more private or more reserved in your sharing than the coaches who share every bit of their process via social media.

Once you determine the right amount of transparency, then do the needed work to get yourself into alignment with your answers. This is examining your beliefs about transparency and sharing and making different decisions about your behaviors. List any limiting beliefs or thoughts you have on this subject. Are they really true? Are they serving you and your clients or are they part of how you are protecting yourself from feeling vulnerable? Conversely, if your business needs you to rein it in a bit, ask yourself why you want to share so much. Are you trying to get attention? Do you have trouble pausing before you shoot off with your thoughts? What would happen if you paused and got grounded before you shared? Could you share in ways that are more sensitive to others?

THOR: H Is for Honest

Authentic marketing is honest. We all know that as a business we cannot make false claims. Yet there are many instances of lying to consumers in order to get sales. Think of the term "snake oil salesman" and you catch my drift. Now we call it "false advertising" and have laws against it. Basically, it means you cannot use false, misleading, or unproven information to promote products/services. You can see this at play with large companies when they get slapped with a lawsuit from the Federal Trade Commission (FTC).

We all get that outright lies should never be used. But what about marketing hype? Can it go too far? For example, some consumers have argued that a campaign like "Red Bull gives you wings" didn't deliver. The complainant received a payout of 13 million dollars in 2014 to settle a case that said Red Bull misled consumers about the superiority of its products with that slogan and its claims of increased performance, concentration, and reaction speed. Although I don't like marketing hype, it seems to me that people should also use common sense in reading marketing messages.

Honesty has taken a beating at the same time our litigious society has beefed up its attacks (for reasons that aren't necessarily tied to honesty!). Today, small business owners aren't sure what they should say—or not say.

It's easier for those offering a product rather than a service. For example, a flower shop owner cannot promise to make your wedding perfect, but they can offer the perfect flowers for your wedding. Toy store owners can claim that childhood can be more fun with the right toys, but not that they can make your child's dreams come true.

When your small business is more personal, made up of only you and your service, you end up dealing with all kinds of issues, not the least of which contains baggage from childhood and society. For example, most of us have been cautioned not to brag, be too full of ourselves, or be too aggressive in sharing our own point of view. After all, we want to be liked by others, don't we? Add to that the fact that your services may be less tangible and more about supporting the customer through a service rather than being a tangible widget. No wonder it feels confusing as to what you can honestly say your services deliver.

Another wrinkle arrived with the internet, which has been less concerned about false advertising rules. Although the FTC has banned false advertising online since the year 2000, it didn't begin cracking down on fake weight loss sites until 2011-13. It wasn't until 2018 that Facebook (FB) and Google began to stop misleading ads when FB came under fire for the false political ads that ran during the Trump/Clinton election. Although we all knew it was happening, there seemed to be little we could do about it. Every person I know has clicked on something that ended up being overblown or hyped, or turned away from the internet in disgust from seeing too much misinformation. This modern phenomenon can turn us off to saying anything at all about our business, afraid we'll come across as pushy or false.

No wonder we're confused.

But here's how transparency and honesty can work together. Try to plainly state as truthfully as you can what you are trying to do for someone. Here are some headlines I came across in my research today:

- Little Known Ways to Save on Your Heating Bill
- Get Rid of That Carpet Stain Once and For All
- Here Is a Method That Is Helping Children Learn to Read Sooner

These headlines say it directly while also creating curiosity. To find these for your business, consider some typical outcomes that have actually happened. Share those. Be direct and uncomplicated in your word choices. Use a sincere, humble, and truthful tone. The headlines above don't sound overly markety, do they? That's because good marketing doesn't have to be clever or gimmicky. I've seen many small businesses do very good business without using any flash. Stick to what's accurate and true, and you'll likely get a good return.

Once you've created dependable and true content for a while, you may want to head toward more creative messaging in your marketing. (I consider this level two marketing and don't believe it's necessary for everyone.) If you're drawn toward creativity, do it well or don't do it. Better to stick to plain than to have fancy messaging that just doesn't work, or worse, misleads people and breaks trust.

Here are some headlines I found online that I consider vague. There's an attempt to be creative, only they don't really say anything specific or clear:

- Creating Excellence In Structural Restoration
- Helping Women on a Mission
- Become a Master Navigator in Your Life
- To Healing Faster, Living Longer, and Achieving Euphoric Mental & Spiritual Balance

Do any of the above evoke your curiosity? Do they make you want to know more about what this person does? Or do you feel slightly confused, like perhaps you should get it but you can't really explain what it's saying? Remember, you will come across in the most authentic way if you just say what needs to be said with the intent of creating understanding.

Here are some headlines that are creative, but also direct enough that they inspire someone to keep reading:

- Go After Your Dreams Like Your Life Depends on It
- How To Quit Your Job (Even When You're Scared Out Of Your Mind)
- No, You Don't Need to be Great at Everything – and Why You Shouldn't Even Try

Don't these evoke an emotional reaction, even if you're not in the market for that particular issue? They are powerful but also direct.

It's not just in headlines that we should aim for honesty blended with creativity. How about when you meet someone new and ask what they do, and they give you some vague answer like "I help people create greater life satisfaction" or "I bring prosperous results to high achieving small business owners." I mean, really, who talks like that? When I meet someone who shares their business in this way, I politely excuse myself from the conversation with an "Oh, how interesting" comment and move on. I know in that moment that this person has not committed to being authentic in their marketing, or may be just unaware, and I have no interest in hearing more.

It's OK to just say what you actually do in your title. That's being both honest and informative. I'm a business and marketing coach. If you are a life or health coach, say that. Ditto for hair stylist, photographer, or weight-loss coach. Are you a personal trainer or consultant? Awesome. Even if you are in network marketing, try to say as simply as you can what you actually do. I would much rather hear that you sell products to maintain healthy skin than that you offer people a glowing lifestyle.

The place you can add a little more creativity comes in your tagline. Here you can speak more directly to the style with which you do something or add some personality about who you do it with. Here are some examples of effective and creative taglines:

- US Postal Service – We deliver
- Travelocity – Wander Wisely
- Lush – Fresh Handmade Cosmetics
- Marie Forleo – The world needs that special gift that only you have

You can see in the above examples that the companies have done a good job of blending honesty with creativity in a way that creates understanding and confidence on the reader's part.

On the other hand, don't downplay what your service

does. Very often I meet talented, intelligent men and women who do amazing work for others, but learned in their early lives to not speak too highly of themselves. They have an inner critic that would stop even the most talented copywriters in their tracks. No wonder those people can't think of what to say about themselves and their work.

If you have to do some inner work to overcome limiting ideas around seeing yourself accurately, do it. That's how you can be honest about yourself. Make an accurate assessment of yourself and the results your work delivers for others and share that.

If you want a tool to help you do this, visit lindabasso.com/authenticmarketer and learn authentic ways to share the brilliance of your work by downloading the worksheet on how to share yours.

Are you honest about what you can really do for your clients? Do you either over or under state your results? Do you find ease in being clear and direct in how you share? If you review your marketing copy and materials, are they informative or unclear?

THOR: O Is For Original

To be authentic, you need to be original. So far so good. But this concept causes all kinds of misunderstandings because the word original means many different things. According to Merriam-Webster, original can mean *a work composed firsthand that from which a copy, reproduction, or translation is made.* It also means *a person with fresh initiative and inventive capacity.* Add to that *the term for a unique or eccentric person.* Our jargon about photocopies and prints of paintings adds even more nuances.

Originally (pun intended) the word meant *the source or cause from which something arises.* Nowhere does it claim that the original has to be the first to arrive at something or the only one working on it. Edison did not invent the light bulb; he was just the first to file a patent. Many people worked to make airplanes fly—not just the Wright brothers. And Rosa Parks wasn't working alone to further the civil rights movement, but rather was part of a whole network of activists working toward this end.

Whether you are the source of an idea or a contributor to its progression doesn't matter. It's enough that you made a unique contribution. Those ideas and efforts are original to you.

Truly there isn't much that hasn't already been done. This is quite the conundrum—unless you went to art school or are involved in the arts. That's where they speak openly about how every artist, writer, or creative fills themselves with others' works to fuel their own inspiration and creative process. I went to art school and remember being amazed at how much time we took in class to study others' works. Sometimes we even recreated another's work so that we could get a glimpse into their process and choice making. By stepping into Picasso or Van Gogh's shoes—and literally trying to copy them—we were turning on our own internal artistic decision-making while building the skill-set we would need to create our own masterpieces. Of course, it would have been wrong to try to sell our copies. But using them to propel our own process forward added to the world of artistic creations, as we were better prepared to make our own contributions.

I wish this concept was more widely taught, but just know that you can do the same by studying those around you who offer work that meets the same needs that you do.

I think this quote from famous filmmaker, Jim Jarmusch, sums it up nicely. And hey, if it's good for the famously creative, maybe there's something there for you too, right?

Nothing is original. Steal from anywhere that resonates with inspiration or fuels your imagination. Devour old films, new films, music, books, paintings, photographs, poems, dreams, random conversations, architecture, bridges, street signs, trees, clouds, bodies of water, light and shadows. Select only things to steal from that speak directly to your soul. If you do this, your work (and theft) will be authentic. Authenticity is invaluable; originality is non-existent. And don't bother concealing your thievery – celebrate it if you feel like it. In any case, always remember what Jean-Luc Godard said: "It's not where you take things from – it's where you take them to." —Jim Jarmusch

If you can drop the idea that learning from others means copying and embrace the idea that the only thing that makes it original comes from your unique stamp on it, you'll experience more ease. Of course, I'm not talking about direct copying, which is illegal and unethical, but digesting another's approach and bringing forth your own version.

This can happen in little or big ways. We were all amazed when Apple came out with the iPod and then the iPhone. They were simply a new take on existing products but with so much originality that they seemed new. But they weren't. The iPod was an upgrade to the Walkman and the iPhone was just a better cell phone.

So look around at your industry, at what and how others are doing something similar to you, at things that inspire you, at what you think works in the world, and what you don't like and let it all wash over you for consideration. Digest all these ideas in your own way so that you can come up with your own point of view. Many times I speak to a new client who wonders how to language something in her marketing and she's trying to do it from a blank slate in her head. I ask what kind of research she's done and the answer comes back as none. After even a few minutes on Google, she has all kinds of ideas of what to say as she reacts to what she agrees with and doesn't in what others are saying.

What you come up with doesn't need to be huge to be original, either. Maybe you have a unique twist on how to use an existing product that could enhance others' lives. Or when you do that YouTube video to explain how you save time in your workday by doing x, y, or z. Little or big, there are many ways to be original in what you are presenting if you allow yourself to step fully into being yourself, digest the world around you, and share in your own way.

The above three (Transparency, Honesty, and Originality) are aspects of authentic marketing that I think are common among the marketing itself for all businesses. Now let's look at how you the owner can step into greater authenticity so that you can find marketing that truly fits your personality and feels good when you do it.

What original contributions are you making with your work? Can you see what makes your business unique? Do you let yourself look at what's out there and digest it to find your own point of view? Or do you have a story that you have to create something from nothing?

THOR: R Is for Real

We hear all the time that you have to be "real" to be authentic. I even used it in the subtitle of this book. What does that mean? After all, most things in the world are real in the sense that they are actual physical objects. But this is only one definition of real.

When used in the context of authenticity, real comes from the informal slang usage of being genuine, having character, or true personality. It may have sprung from the phrase "the real McCoy" coined in the late 1800s. Whatever it comes from, its meaning comes across clearly: the genuine article trumps the fake one.

Good news! Being a solopreneur or small company makes being real easier. You just have to step away from your training or belief that marketing has to be clever or say something different and express yourself the way you would naturally would.

Often potential clients come to me and say, "I don't know what to say in my marketing materials." When I ask them to tell me about their business, they say some lovely things about what they do. I tell them, "That was perfect."

Their eyes widen a little, and they ask incredulously "It is? I thought I needed to say it better or differently or like so-and-so does. It sounds so (fill in the blank with some negative descriptor) the way I say it."

They often have a whole host of reasons why what they told me couldn't possibly be good enough: it doesn't seem polished, they weren't sure it sounded good, they were afraid they hadn't explained it well. By downplaying how they would say something, or not letting their own words be enough, they are literally telling themselves that who they are is not good enough. In other words, they are denying their own authenticity!

Not that I'm saying it's easy. We grow up in a culture that doesn't encourage us to be ourselves. We are marketed at constantly by "lifestyle" brands that basically tell us we will be happy if we follow the trends rather than our own guiding star. Our culture can be competitive, and we learn from an early age that winning should be aspired to. Even our biology lessons in school affirm this with the interpretation of Darwin's survival of the fittest as the reason for our species' very survival. I don't see many messages to children that they should find their own path and follow it to the feeling of having enough.

I see many more messages around having more, doing

more, and coming out on top, which creates an atmosphere of comparing our progress to another's and looking for that outside mechanism—be it clothing, schools, or some group or another—that can get us there. We end up taking on roles like daughter or son, student, employee, partner, and parent to do what we think we are supposed to do rather than looking for our own genuine version of living our lives.

Constantly comparing leads you to live a life of "roles" rather than one of authenticity

---

Growing up in this way can make it hard to find our real selves when we step into the role of business owner. But find it we must because the businesses that embrace "real" do better business.

What does it mean to be a real girl small business owner? In general, it means choosing a business that feels like a good fit for who you really are. You cannot work in a business because others think it would be a good idea, or even that there's a lot of money to be made, unless it dovetails with *your* needs. You have to do your business in a way that reflects your actual inner truths and perspectives, even if it means going against the grain of what's traditionally done.

I see this often with small business owners exhausting themselves with traditional business hours when they are better suited to starting work late, or should work sporadically when they have energy. Do you have to find a way to run your business that's attractive and convenient for your clients? Yes. Do you have to do it the way it's always been done in that industry even if that doesn't work for you? No. Our businesses and the way we do them generally have more flexibility than we suppose they do.

Here are common areas where I see small business owners

not being "real" in their businesses:

- **Type of business you run:** Maybe you fell into your business, taking what popped up or fell into your lap. Or it seemed like the natural next step because of your skill set, what you were doing before, or it was a popular choice, but you dream of doing something else. You may feel the other business would be lovely to do "but…" and the reasons why you can't, or how far away those options are start popping up. The gap between where you are and doing that seems immense. Or maybe you are in a business or industry that doesn't seem to fit your personality. Perhaps you are in a business that needs a lot of sales attention or forces you to be with lots of other people and it drains your energy because you are an introvert. Or it's a business that would do well with a big social media presence and you hate the online world. However it shows up, there's a definite mismatch between you and the business you run, and it's hard to see how you could shift it. There may be other ways that you or your business don't come together, but the theme here is owners who believe they cannot be in a business that accommodates their real preferences.

- **Hours you work:** Some businesses come with certain hours that may not fit how we are designed. Financial markets demand early morning phone calls if you are on the west coast. Store hours mean long stretches during the day. A hospitality business means working weekends and holidays. The hours of your business affect not only each day of your life, but also the flow of your year. Maybe your busiest season happens when you are also personally busiest with family obligations. Or you are slow at times when you really need cash to come in. Can these be changed? Sometimes yes, though when it's no, there are often tweaks you can make or ways to get shored up for the times that don't personally work for you. Getting real about the times you like to work and don't is the difference

between spending a lot of time in your zone of genius and feeling depleted by your business.
- **Timing of work:** Besides the overall business you run, there's the day-to-day existence within your open hours. I often see small business owners who don't time their workdays well and end up not getting done what they need to and feeling frazzled and unaccomplished. It's a vicious cycle as each day continues getting away from them as the inner criticism and anxiety mount. It leads you to feeling like something is wrong with you. This happens by letting clients interrupt any time instead of having ways to contact you and times to work with you that fit the rest of your schedule, not having good to-do lists or calendaring systems, overcommitting to please others, and not scheduling blocks of time that work with your personal rhythms. You simply must get real with yourself about what you actually need during your days and weeks to move your business along. Being constantly buried or behind the eight ball are not mandatory in running your own business. Drop that old habit and step into new ways of managing your business that truly support you.
- **Activities in their business:** It's common to see entrepreneurs not doing activities that make their hearts sing but rather that they feel they "have" to. This often looks like saying yes to something that you have a bad feeling about because you need the money or think the project is a stepping stone to somewhere else. Then you are stuck doing a whole lot of things you'd rather not. It also often goes poorly because your heart isn't really in it and additional headaches get piled on. Or it looks like pursuing marketing efforts that you don't really want to do, like networking when you'd rather not or sitting in your office working on ads or other technical things that drive you crazy. Yes, there are a whole bunch of things that typically have to happen within your business and many of

those things may not be fits for you. Get out of thinking that you have to do them anyway. Many times there are choices within the have tos. Like in marketing, there are almost always options or ways to do things differently enough to accommodate personal preferences. And various parts of our business can and should be outsourced so that we aren't the only doers in our business. The only thing I don't recommend is trying to do it all yourself. Your strengths cannot possibly cover all aspects of your business because no one's can. Get real about what you like and don't and make decisions accordingly.

- **People you serve:** last but surely not least are the types of people you work with. This ranges from the clients you take on to the vendors you hire to the communities your business exists within. Finding a good fit in all of these areas is necessary for you to have a business that totally fits you. Why would you take on clients who don't light you up or that you struggle to serve? The reasons can range from having a habit of people pleasing to mistakenly believing that you are not good enough to just not realizing that you have a choice. You do and you must exercise it in order to create alignment in your business. When you work with clients who are good fits for your business, it creates a magical dynamic where they are happy, you are happy, and beautiful work gets done. Work for the wrong folks and just the opposite happens. Ditto for vendors or the communities your business exists in. Good things often come from what feels good, and rarely do good things come from what feels bad.

You will read more about being your whole self in chapter 3. For now, trust me that being real matters.

For larger companies that are not closely run by one or two owners, being real can be trickier as the company isn't directly connected to the owners. These companies are generally groups of people that have come together to provide some product or service in exchange for money. It comes from someone needing to earn a living, inventing a way to do that, and growing it to a point where it employs numbers of people to fulfill the product or service. Sometimes a company like this has no deeper purpose than earning money. In this case, I don't advise making up a brand and trying to give it a personality. This is insulting and part of the reason marketing can feel distasteful.

For instance, if you do your due diligence in looking inward with the management team and employees and don't find a deeper core reason for being in business, then look to your product or the spirit of the person who founded it. Apple did a fine job of branding itself solely around its innovative nature. Consider if your company was founded in response to a problem happening at a certain time in history, or if the founder had a vision that there are still threads of in the company today. Look beyond the obvious reasons your business exists to the underlying themes that may be there until you find something real to build your brand from.

If you are in the business only to make money, then consider having a strong charitable arm to your business instead of promoting yourself as a caring people company. Use cause marketing as a way to connect. In this way, your company is being real, in effect saying: You give us money and we, in turn, share some of it with others either by employing them or donating to causes that support an important need. That's much better than creating some disingenuous marketing campaign positioning your company as a warm, fuzzy people place.

I'm not saying that money is anti-people. I'm saying that you cannot make up something from a PR or marketing angle that isn't real and expect it to work.

Some companies were originally founded for a deeper

reason at a time when being real about that reason wasn't encouraged. For example, prior to Facebook and Millennials coming into the workforce, there was a notion that business and personal lives should be kept separate. This meant that no one wanted to hear why you started your business. Now, many of those businesses are larger companies that lack the realness factor increasingly desired by consumers.

In this case, it's possible to excavate the real aspect of your business and bring that into your brand. You usually have to go back to the original aims of the founder, or spend time understanding what's unique about the culture that has grown within the company since founding. You need to do some work to understand what personality your company has and how your brand can be real to someone.

This is a process that includes a brand evaluation, i.e., looking at both internal and external perceptions, doing a competitive brand and customer analysis, and completing a brand re-development. At this point, it's usually not possible to do this with your internal team and means bringing in an outside agency to assist.

In reading the above, could you say that yes, you are being real in all the areas covered by THOR? Are there areas where you need to make improvements? What holds you back from being your real self in these areas? Are you afraid you'll be rejected or lose business? How would it feel to be really real in your business?

What Gets in the Way of Authenticity?

So far I've shared the traits that I believe make your marketing authentic. That's just the beginning of the story. As solopreneurs or small business owners, we are present in our businesses in many more ways than just some traits that show up in marketing. Some go so far as to say that for us microbusinesses, we ourselves are our brands. In which case, the authenticity has to come through on many levels for our business to truly fit us. The rest of this book takes a look at this fact and gives strategies and tools for how to become more authentic within your business and make it visible. Heck, it may even spillover into your life. That's just the point. It's really being your whole self in your business that lets you be an authentic marketer. Let's start by looking at what may get in the way of that happening.

This book got started when a very earnest entrepreneur asked me just *how* she could be authentic in *her* marketing. I froze for a second as my brain computed new information. This woman was asking me *how* she could be *her* in her marketing. I was caught in my own thoughts as I thought about how to answer her. She was, after all, sitting in front of me presumably being *her* in this moment. And I'm guessing she is generally *her* in the work she does for her clients.

Part of why I froze came from being stuck in the past. As I mentioned earlier, in the first 18 years of my career, I had worked for much larger clients. Authenticity in marketing was always about convincing those in management that it was the correct thing to do. I was coming at it from the place of convincing others to do it. Instead, this woman showed me that for a small business with only one or a few individuals something else happens. The people in these businesses long to bring their authenticity forward, but facing a sea of marketing tactics that seem disingenuous and hyped, they aren't sure how to go about that. We've grown up in an era where marketing has meant "dressing something up" to sell. We've been told that our success will come from how well we "package" our services, "brand" our identity, or "deliver" our message. No wonder we aren't sure what that means for us solopreneurs or heads of communities. We ARE undeniably human with contradictions, messy emotions, and lots of mystery. Given that, we ARE NOT sure just how to stuff that into the right package. Add the pressure of needing that pretty package to sell for our very livelihood, and bingo, there's the question of exactly HOW that's supposed to go.

Here's some good news: Authentic marketing is not the package, but rather what's inside the package. It's about who you are being rather than what you are doing. This means it's accessible to us all when we are just ourselves.

Authentic marketing comes from who you are rather than what you do

---

For most of us, when we feel settled, happy, and confident, we feel fine just being ourselves. It's when we aren't sure about the way we are and whether that will work for the situation at hand that we start trying on roles or scrambling to understand how to "be" in this situation. In other words, we move away from *being* and focus on *doing*. The real question then becomes not how to be authentic, but rather what's in your way of being yourself.

The Need to Belong

We are wired as humans in ways that can confuse the search for our real selves.

On one hand, research shows that humans have a fundamental need to belong. This need seems to be evolutionary and when not met causes ill effects such as emotional negativity, increased stress, lowered immune systems, higher death rates, and greater amounts of mental illness. People deprived of a sense of belonging are highly prone to a spread of behavioral problems, which range from traffic accidents to criminality to suicide.[1]

The need to belong drives us to behave in ways to fit in. As early as 3 years old, we seek to cooperate with others and form groups. From that age forward, we attach easily to groups and try to match our behaviors to that of the group. Even subtle cues from the group influence our behavior, and we remain in them even if it costs us personally.[2] In research settings, this happens when the groups we are in are randomly assigned, filled with complete strangers, or even with previously disliked others. We resist the breaking of our bonds even when there are practical and material reasons for doing so.[3]

On the other end of the spectrum, we have a need for autonomy, or determining for ourselves what we do and how we do something. This is considered to be a critical psychological need, necessary for optimal growth and a sense of wellbeing. When someone has it, they feel engaged and happy. When they don't, they can feel alienated, helpless, and even hostile.[4]

The rub comes in that although all people will strive for this capacity to decide for themselves, regardless of culture or background, having autonomy is linked to the environment we are in and whether that environment supports it. Put another way, the well being of any individual depends on how much the environment they are in provides opportunities to satisfy this need for autonomy.[5]

Our wellbeing is linked to having the opportunity to be our true selves

---

Can you see the dilemma? We are all striving for something—to be our own selves—and we feel better when we find it. We also have this primal need to belong to groups and the expectations and demands of these groups determine whether we get to express our desire to be ourselves or conform to the group. In some sense, your personal expression ends up being determined by the environment you find yourself in. No wonder we don't always find our authenticity.

Jessica grew up in a liberal area of the country, though her family and friends looked with suspicion at those who did anything too "woo-woo", including natural healing, spiritual practices, or energy work. Jessica was drawn to those belief systems, which left her in a tough spot. How could she fit in with the people around her when they hated the things that she found so amazing? In her younger years, she ignored their call to her. Instead, she partied with the people around her, pretending as though she couldn't care less about healing, self-growth, and how we are connected energetically to our environment. Though she felt glad to be a part of her community, this approach led her to feel alienated from herself, and by her college years, she developed a drug and weight problem.

When she moved away from her hometown, she was able to drop the addiction, manage her weight, and her interests slowly began emerging in ways that she could engage with. She felt happier for herself but often felt guilty in pursuing these personal passions, wondering what her childhood friends or her family would think. In her head, she could hear their voices teasing her even though they were hundreds of miles away. Ten years into owning her own business, she's been called to various training programs that have given her the skills she's always longed to have in order to work with her clients in ways that manage their energy, focus on self-care, and help with addictions.

But if you look at her marketing materials, none of this approach shows up. Even though she's taking the steps to get the training, and using it with her clients with success, she cannot find peace with this path. She cannot say out loud that she's doing this type of work. In fact, when she talks about her work, she still jokes that it's "woo-woo whacky stuff," rather than expressing what she loves about it. If Jessica could step more fully into the pain she feels about growing up somewhere that didn't accept her for who she was so that she could more fully accept herself now, she could find more ease in her own skin—and in her own business.

Other Reasons

In my work, clients come to me to do their marketing in ways that feel right for them. Over the years of working with these folks, I've come to see similarities in the reasons they don't feel good about marketing or are trying to find a different way to do it.

What can trample your enjoyment of marketing?

1. You see it as cheesy, salesy, hyped, or icky.
2. You are trying to use someone else's system and it's not a fit for you.
3. Your nervous system reacts to your visibility.

In order to do marketing that feels good, we need to reframe these issues. It's simply not possible to keep coming at it from one of these perspectives and expect that authenticity will shine through. Even if there's a kernel of truth in each of these, we need to root them out and deal with them. Keeping them in this limited form just doesn't serve.

Let's start with the first one. If you are approaching your marketing with the belief that it's somehow unsavory or bad, you are more likely to avoid doing it. When you choose to look at marketing through the lens of what can go wrong within it, you limit your ability to do it. Why not try a different lens? As we discussed earlier, marketing can be looked at as a profound act of service. If you're not there yet, you could at least start with an attitude that it may not be your most favorite business activity, but you are willing to work on it in order to serve more people. Of course, there is some truth that marketing can be any of these things if not done well. But let that be a lesson to you on what to avoid in yours. Find your authenticity rather than stopping before your start.

The second hindrance—not being a good fit—comes up often for the entrepreneurs I work with. When we start our businesses, we often need to gain new skills. Naturally we look around for advice and knowledge to support us. Here's where things often go awry. Most of us have a decision-making ability that's tied to our conditioning rather than our authenticity. We follow advice from people who we would never consider letting into our personal lives because they are too aggressive, fake, and always in sales mode. Still, we think their business advice must be just what we need, even though it feels terrible to implement it. We often get paralyzed in our business by all the "shoulds" we have rolling around that came to us from an outside source and we feel conflicted about. Instead, we choose to do nothing.

Or instead of taking in information and deciding whether it truly works for us or not, we take in information we assume we have to follow—even if it doesn't fit. We are so conditioned by our upbringing to listen to authority and experts that we often don't even question them. An expert tells us that we have to post on social media 8x/day, and we cover our eyes in despair and then exhaust ourselves with mediocre postings. Or avoid doing it altogether.

What we need to do is find someone we respect and admire, who's had success in their business in a way that we believe fits us, and learn to build our skills from them but in a way that's personalized to us. We have to apply the same level of decision-making that's made our personal lives successful to our business decisions. I work with all my clients to create a solid decision-making skill-set that lets them make good decisions about their marketing *without* me. If you do the same, you can experience a lot more of *you* in your marketing efforts rather than all those pesky shoulds and rather nots that can accumulate.

The third one seems quite unusual for a marketing and business coach to address. What does our nervous system have to do with our ability to be authentic in our business? We humans are literally a bundle of nerves wrapped in a body. The nervous system includes our brain, spinal cord, and all the nerves that run from there throughout the body. It's responsible for managing most of what we consider living such as movement, balance, coordination, breathing, our heartbeat, sleep, hunger, thirst, digestion, reproductive health, aging, perception, thoughts, emotions, learning, memory, and even how we deal with stress. There is literally nothing that you do in your marketing that won't be registered by your nervous system.

As we grow up, we store all kinds of responses to the world in our nervous system. This acts as a means to either protect us from similar bad experiences from happening or to help us find similar good experiences. The part that doesn't work for our marketing comes from the fact that sometimes we've registered these experiences incorrectly. For example, we may have registered that being visible will mean being ridiculed, being rejected, or worse, cause danger. Or we conclude that pretending to be somebody we're not is the best way to gain acceptance from others. These can definitely get in the way of being all of you in your visibility efforts.

If you are having trouble with being authentic in your business or getting visible in ways that get results, look to these four areas to find where you need to enact a fix:

HOW YOU ARE DESIGNED	LIMITING BELIEFS
LACK OF INNER PERMISSION	OLD DYSFUNCTION

We'll look at each of these in more detail and at how you can fix these areas in the chapters to come. For now, let me explain them briefly.

HOW YOU ARE DESIGNED: This is the way you're uniquely put together. It includes your personality, preferences, quirks, heart and soul desires, and all those bits that make you the YOU that you are. Getting down to the real you is needed if you want to share it with the world. First, you have to discover it. Second, you have to deeply accept it. Some parts of us we love and other parts we do not. Authenticity means knowing and accepting it all.

LIMITING BELIEFS: These are those pesky thoughts that flit through your mind rehashing outdated beliefs, old ways of thinking, and stories that you've unknowingly picked up along the way. In your business your beliefs are either helping or hurting your ability to grow. The old adage that "if you think you can't, you're right" encapsulates this idea well. Getting your beliefs to support you, rather than hinder, is our goal.

LACK OF INNER PERMISSION: We grow up with social and cultural norms that shape our perspective. These are the "rules" by which our lives are governed and are often historical rather than conscious. Examples include how women or men are supposed to behave, what good people do/don't do, what God/religious rules demand, and the many rules around politics, money, race, gender, and the power we hold. Unexamined these run our lives, including how we show up in our businesses, according to belief systems that may not even match our own points of view, or support our hopes for a new direction. We have to find the permission inside ourselves to move forward boldly and in ways that fit the real us.

OLD DYSFUNCTION: At an earlier time in our lives we may have been in an accident, had trauma, or dealt with a high level of stress from a dysfunctional situation we found ourselves in. As I explained above, these experiences get stored in our nervous systems. They often get inadvertently stirred up when we go toward being more visible in our businesses, because of the risk and vulnerability we feel in becoming more visible. This happens to even the most accomplished business people and even to those who've already done a tremendous amount of personal growth or therapeutic work on these old wounds. In order to grow our businesses, sometimes we have to revisit these situations, clean them up, and get free from them internally.

Questions for Reflection:
- Which of the THOR traits of authentic marketing come easiest for you: being transparent, honest, original, or real?
- In which of the THOR traits of authentic marketing do you need to step more fully?
- Is your need for belonging at odds with you being yourself in your business?
- Do you have any of the other blocks mentioned to being your full self within your business?

There's clearly a lot that goes into being our authentic selves. Remember, any journey that leads to great outcomes has many steps. It's not as important that you arrive at the end point as it is that you get on the path. Any number of steps you take toward being more of your authentic self in your business can increase your sense of ease. Having walked far down this path, I can say that the outcomes far outweigh any efforts you need to take. Let's look at some specific ways you can head down this pathway toward your own authenticity.

3

BE YOUR WHOLE SELF

See Your Unique Design

Personality, preferences, and the stage of life you are in should all be part of how you decide your approach to marketing. I often see introverts struggling with marketing plans better suited for extroverts, parents of young children wishing to launch a 6-figure business while staying home with their children, or a retiree who on one hand wants to slow down and on the other wants to start a new business.

Am I saying these things can't be done? No, but I am saying these contradictions in life stage, personality, and preferences make the marketing efforts much more difficult. If you are willing to consider all of you in planning your marketing, I find enacting the plan goes much more smoothly.

Your preference considerations include:
- Your personal rhythms

- Activities you like/dislike doing
- How much/often you want to work
- Environment you like to work in

You may not have ever considered one or more of these in your work before. Maybe you always thought that work happened between 9am-5pm even if your personal energy is highest at 6am. Or maybe you assume that you have to do all parts of your business, even your most dreaded tasks that drain your energy. I have a colleague who worked at his kitchen table for more than a year. He didn't want to bother with setting up an office in part of his guest room, because it would prompt a difficult conversation with his wife about his upcoming move from his full-time job to his new business that he was sure she did not support. Needless to say, his business didn't go very far that first year as he was constantly interrupted. Once he made the move to claim his office space, his work flowed much faster!

Your personality considerations include:

Whether you are an introvert or extrovert: This is not about shyness or whether you feel OK walking up to new people. An introvert's energy gets drained when they spend time with others, and gets refilled when they spend time alone. Extroverts are opposite. This should play into your marketing decisions as an extrovert should not spend hours alone at their computer, say writing articles or setting up tech stuff for a campaign. If they do have to do "alone" type tasks, they may do better if they do it in a place that has people such as a café or co-work space. An introvert might feel energized after working alone for a few hours but may get drained after speaking or attending an event. It's not to say that either type can't do things that drain them, but setting up a marketing strategy that takes advantage of your energy system will be the easiest to implement and likely to flow.

Where you have influence: We all have the ability to influence certain types of people. Think about the types of people you know. Who reaches out to you to ask your advice and who do you feel most comfortable spending time with? When you are seated in serving those you are able to influence with ease, your marketing happens more easily. For instance, I had a client work with me briefly who wanted to help people in transition from one job to another. But she had no connections to people in Human Resources, job fairs, job skill training programs, or anyone else that regularly interacted with folks making these kinds of transitions. In fact, she didn't even know many people who worked at typical company jobs as she mostly associated with other entrepreneurs. She had no influence with people in job transitions. In the meantime, she was literally surrounded by women whose children were leaving home and were making the transition from mothering to building a new chapter in their lives. They asked her for advice, took walks with her, and invited her to their social events. Can you guess which of these two groups of people she has more influence with? If she was willing to create products or services for those women who were experiencing transition, then her marketing would be easier for her to do. Can you create influence with a new group of people that you currently don't have influence with? Yes, but it takes conscious effort and time to do so. You would have to identify where they are and take action to become part of their community and to get to know folks so that you can build influence. Making those efforts would be the first part of your marketing plan.

Who you feel called to serve: Working with the wrong people can make your business feel hard and decrease your confidence. I often see small business owners avoid narrowing their audience to their ideal client because they don't want to exclude anyone. This breaks my heart because trying to work for everyone means that no one wins. Technically, you can probably do your business for many different types of people. But there are some that you have more ease, more connection, and a greater fit with. This leads to them getting more from your work and you enjoying the time you spend with them. It makes it easier to do your marketing because you are talking to a specific type of person. This is not about exclusion. It's about creating so much love and connection for a single type of person that everyone is best served. Not doing this would be a little like telling yourself to get romantically involved with anyone who needed you, or anyone that made "sense" to be involved with. It's not how the heart works in romance, nor in choosing great clients for our businesses.

Your quirks: We all have those quirky things that make up all of who we are. Maybe it makes sense for you to work with a certain type of person but you just don't want to. Or you have a loud laugh and you're in a quiet industry. Or you like good old-fashioned pen and paper and avoid using digital tools even though they would be faster. Whatever yours are, own them and consciously bring them into your business in ways that work for you, rather than against. Don't cringe, get embarrassed or think that your quirks are weird. They probably are, and that's beautiful. This is about being the real you, not trying to hide your bits and pieces which can drain your energy and make you appear inauthentic. You will do best when you fit your business around the real you, not the other way round.

Finally, **consider your stage of life.** Business advice is not one size fits all. That's why it can be so difficult to read an article and enact what they are suggesting that you do. It may be that the advice is not a good fit for your personality or your personal preferences. It also could be that the advice is not aimed at someone in your stage of life. When you are just getting started in your 20's, you cannot benefit from advice aimed at midlife parent business owners. Ditto for work at home moms who are reading how tech startups in Silicon Valley market themselves. The same goes for later midlife folks who are starting their business as their second act. Maybe you used to be the picture of health and are now dealing with an ongoing condition, or you suddenly have loads of time since your children left for college. Each stage of life brings with it particular responsibilities, tendencies, demands and amounts of energy.

Things to factor into your marketing plan about your stage of life include:

- The decade of life you're in. As your 20's tend to differ from 30's differ from 40's, and on down the line, each decade seems to call forth different qualities from us.
- Your life experience. Whatever your age, some have experienced little in regards to their proposed business and some a lot.
- Your health and what you do to maintain it. This pertains to how much stress you can take, the hours you have available for your business, whether you can travel or are a homebody, etc.
- Energy you have available (mental, emotional, physical, spiritual) to put toward your marketing, to deal with other people, to take on new skillsets, and to handle setbacks.
- Commitments you have to others like marriage, partnerships, children, aging parents, communities, professional organizations, etc. as these impact your time and energy available for your business.
- Your financial status. Most businesses take 3-5 years to really flourish with steady sales. Of course, you will

make money along the way but you will also need to invest money. Having a safety net while you start your business will dictate certain marketing steps while not having one will call others into play.

You should also consider the intangible design you were born with. Look to a system of typing people like Human Design, Enneagram, Kolbe, or StrengthsFinder. These systems identify the individual way you were created. This ensures your plan takes into account how you are designed.

I like to use a car analogy with my clients. If you are designed to be a Porsche but you are moving through your life trying to do the heavy work of a diesel truck, or vice versa, you are probably not getting the best out of yourself, or the situations you are involved in. When you understand your unique design, you can take advantage of your inborn strengths and bolster your weak spots.

Let's look at the Human Design System as an example. This system can help you understand the best way to network and make yourself more visible. A projector, one of the three types in the system that makes up only about 21% of the population, must be recognized by another, rather than approach someone directly. A generator type, which is 70% of us, must feel a pull or response toward someone before we can approach them. And a manifestor, which only describes 8% of people, can approach anyone, though they have better results if they inform others while they do it. There are, of course, many nuances in someone's Human Design chart that I've skipped here, but I'm just trying to share the essence to make the point. The projectors would do best at the event if someone else who knew them introduced them around. The generators would be well served to hang back for a moment and see who they had a response to before approaching anyone. The manifestors could approach anyone they like, although because their design flows best when they inform others before they take an action, they would do best if they started off by letting the other person know, like starting the conversation with "Hi, I'm stopping by to introduce myself, if that's okay" instead of just sticking out their hand for a shake and saying their name with no preamble.

Since these three designs have vastly different approaches, you would need to know your design first in order to create a successful connection at the networking event. I've seen many other traits in individual people's Human Design that orient them to make the most success in their businesses including how they make the most accurate decisions, where their strengths are, how to work best with others, and even how to get new business.

Knowing your design doesn't only make you more effective. It helps you bring your whole self to your marketing. We've moved past the time in our culture when it's OK to only bring a slice of yourself to your marketing efforts—to just say what you do and hope people buy. The transparency required in today's marketing to bring the right clients to you comes when you bring your whole self. This means accepting how you are actually designed, not how you wish you were.

A midlife man with a ton of business and mindfulness experience, Jeff was ready to put his work out into the world in a bigger way. He created his signature coaching program and started looking for candidates. He came to me to help him fill this program with students (yes, I work with a few good men, too!) When we looked at his Human Design, several things stood out. One is that he is designed to get work by waiting to see what life brings to him rather than chasing an opportunity and he is designed to have "down" times when nothing is happening. He also is designed to bring change about on an enterprise level, which is more of a consulting than coaching type of role.

In my opinion, Jeff's main work in getting new business was to step back and be patient. Instead of chasing down new opportunities (which is what he had been doing and wasn't experiencing success with) he spent some time acknowledging that indeed the world had always brought him the correct opportunities when he was patient and managed his doubts and fears about being supported. He also stepped into his acceptance that his communication skills and ability to follow his instincts to create success for others is not trivial but actually quite profound, and makes him an excellent business consultant. Because these skills came naturally to him, he had been downplaying them as not that great.

Within weeks of reviewing his Human Design, opportunities began coming to Jeff as he started accepting this new knowledge of himself. Some of his coaching clients began asking him to step into bigger roles within their organization. Within three months, he had a large consulting engagement in place and more satisfying relationships with his private coaching clients. By the end of one year, his income was doubled, he had a large corporate client, and he was much more visible within his professional community. It wasn't all easy as the "down" times in his chart where nothing seemed to be happening were difficult to deal with. Jeff has had to learn to love the times when things are moving forward with ease and to manage the times that are not, because they are part of how he's designed, not something that can be changed. Finally, he is now offering his signature coaching course and writing a book for his corporate clients that he has found are the correct fit for his influence. Overall, he found a much more satisfying way of working with others that brings to life his core skillset.

Have you ever wondered how all these various typing systems were developed? Some swear by their astrology, some by their Enneagram number, and others by their StrengthsFinder profile. Carl Jung endorsed the channeled Human Design system, which set the stage for the Meyers-Briggs system. The Enneagram can be traced through Sufi, Judaic, and Christian lineages. Outside consultants have built a plethora of their own systems such as Lance Secretan's 5Dynamics or Steve Faktor's Nine Corporate Personas. In Ivy League graduate studies programs, students are required to assess themselves with the Meyers-Briggs or other personality team assessment tools. Corporations create their own tests or buy one of many types of enterprise level of assessments that include cognitive ability, personality, and even integrity tests. There are many types of assessments, and they come from various points of view, including intellectual, psychological, and even spiritual points of view. How can all of these be right? How do you know which to use?

From my perspective, each has something to offer, and it's about finding the one that resonates with you. In other words, the one that helps *you* understand *yourself*. Each person who has created one of these systems has seen a glimpse of the overall universal design and created a system that brings to life some of the pieces, in ways that made sense to them. Some have divined the whole system; others have based it on observation. Neither approach ranks as better or worse, and both have value. Something can be learned from each system that has been developed. In my experience, even if you look to several different systems, you will still see commonalities and complimentary references of your personality, as they all paint a picture of you.

We have a society that doesn't value individuation, a term Carl Jung coined for the process of living into your individual personality. Culturally, we don't practice tools of self-inquiry in a way that leads to approaching the world through our own unique lens. Vision quests and coming-of-age rituals traditionally held this place, allowing people to begin to know themselves deeply while still participating or finding their place within the tribe. Conversely, in our consumer capital-based system, many of us have learned to fit in, rather than find our unique skill-set.

You must seek systems that resonate with you to understand yourself and your design. This is not frivolous or self-indulgent. Knowing oneself used to be a high calling. People spent their lifetime trying to understand their own nature. Now we hurl ourselves forward so fast through time that we barely remember to breathe, let alone contemplate the deeper nature of ourselves.

Nor can you use the investigation of yourself as an avoidance mechanism or distraction. Many purpose-driven entrepreneurs keep learning more and more about themselves, seeking system after system. But it's really not to deeply know themselves; rather, they are looking for a quick fix or use it as a distraction from doing real growth work. It would be fine to explore some number of systems with the intent of finding the one or two you want to study and apply over time. In diving more deeply, you can gain true understanding of the real you. The goal of this exploration should not be to explain away your behavior, or to feel better about the things you do. It's to learn more about your own motivations, inklings, and weaknesses to be more accepting of your real self. This knowledge and acceptance is the pathway to authenticity.

In truth, we are all here to do something different and it makes us unlike anyone else. We all have a deep personal well of power, but may not realize it as we strive to fit in and be acceptable to others. For instance, some of you have the power of fighting the status quo, or of being individually oriented to learn about the human collective. This might cause some clash as our society dictates that we all be social when some of us are actually not designed to be. Your power may not feel like a power at all in the society in which you find yourself! Do not doubt how you were designed. You must go from the assumption that you were designed this way for a reason. Find it and act on it if you want to experience the most ease in your life.

We've also come to believe that we can change ourselves or become a better version of who we are. Nothing could be further from the truth. This pursuit will cause you great pain as you deny your very nature in favor of fashion or outside opinion. You must find the systems you have resonance with, study them, and apply them to your lives, all with the focus of finding the real parts of you. Finding unsavory parts or difficult parts may not feel easy, but this path doesn't promise ease. You must learn to admit truth even when it seems painful to do so. It can be much more painful to suppress it. Admitting it only stings in the beginning and then gets integrated into your strength of being.

I know because I've been on this journey myself. I've studied many systems and learned a great deal about myself, both good and bad. At one point, I learned from studying Claudio Naranjo, a Chilean psychologist who presented an interpretation of the Enneagram that I am vain, selfish, and cruel. Was this easy for me to really admit? Heck no, even though I know deep down I really do have these qualities as part of me. It was heartbreaking, as I really have spent a big part of my life trying hard to be the opposite of these things. It still causes me to feel uncomfortable, and I don't go out of my way to dwell on it for sure! But somehow, I can say I am also stronger for knowing this. It gives me a depth that people respond to. I'm often told how real I seem. It is also humbling for me, and helps me more quickly resolve situations when any of these traits come to the surface. Since I'm not in denial of them, it's easier for me to see them and admit them so that they pass through, rather than cause a lot of drama. I have much more control of them than I would if I was suppressing them.

Being honest about your shortcomings does not make them stronger, as many fear. It's not in naming your weaknesses that they grow. Instead, when you admit them, it puts you in a conscious relationship with them—one that gives you more choice and greater control of your actions.

The better you can come to know yourself, the more of you that can truly show up in your business. It makes it easier to create a realistic plan for yourself and your business. By considering the real you, there's a better chance your plan will be realistic to what you can do.

Questions for Reflection:

- In what ways can your personality, preferences, or stage of life shape the marketing that you do?
- Are you honoring your personal preferences when you decide what types of marketing fit you?
- Do you spend time trying to get to know the real you?
- Have you studied systems that increase your knowledge of yourself? Why or why not?

Know Your Worth

It's not enough to just know ourselves well; we need to go deeper. How? We need to fundamentally BE ourselves. By this I mean our real selves, not the false self we may have developed to defend against our hurts or our lack of acceptance by others. Back to our car analogy, if you were a diesel truck born into a family or culture of Porsches, you wouldn't grow up feeling as though that was a good thing. Like the proverbial ugly duckling story, the baby swan doesn't feel beautiful in a group that comes down on it for not being a duck.

At the core, it's about even more than sharing your real self with others in your visibility. It's about the gift of getting to BE your own self at an intimate level. The more you can accept yourself for who you really are, who you really came here to be, the more settled in your own skin you'll be. That quality not only attracts prospective clients, but it also makes you more successful overall. How many of us strive to feel more worthy or not feel like an imposter? Self-acceptance is the core healing for both of these.

Self-acceptance is the core of your authenticity

To accept yourself, you must believe in your own worth. Thinking you are not worthy may be the bane of human existence—believing the things outside yourself define who you are, or that feedback from others can impact who you are truly. Spiritually and energetically, nothing could be further from the truth. But in modern life, we don't seem to be taking that in. Low self worth, self esteem issues, perfectionism, confidence gap, self doubt, self-sabotage, body image issues, and imposter syndrome are words we use to talk about the ways in which we girls end up feeling less than OK about ourselves and our capabilities.

It's Not Just You

Here may be some good news. We all have these kinds of doubts about ourselves. Today, online articles say that an estimated 70% of adults have experienced that feeling of not being capable despite their past achievements, or believing that this time, someone is going to tap them on the shoulder and say they've figured out they're a fraud. This spreads across men, women, high achievers, and students. But I will tell you that 100% of the people I know have experienced these issues in the past or still have them. Most high achievers I know express they have continuing doubts despite their growing list of accomplishments. If the people we perceive to be rocking it feel this way, why would we be surprised that we average folks have it?

The reasons why we come to feel like this are varied but I bet you'll recognize at least one of these that fits.

- **Those critical voices:** criticism comes in many forms and sometimes in such sneaky ways that we don't even recognize we are getting, or giving, it. Of course, there are the outright critical people who may have been in our early lives. The parent who spoke harshly in response to us or even called us belittling things. No child can grow up with hostile adults around them or be called stupid, fat, lazy, dumb, etc. without questioning what's wrong with them when they are older. Maybe that one is obvious. But there's also the parent, coach, or other adults who constantly questioned our decisions with phrases like "wouldn't that be better if you…" type sentiments. Or there is the adult who means to cheer you on but it comes out like, "Hey, that was great! But if you could just adjust your shot like this then you'd really be…" type suggestions. Always questioning someone else's decisions or suggesting a better way for them to do it robs them of learning from their experience and makes them feel constantly unsure of their actions. Of course, it's not just a problem in our childhoods. The way human biology works is that we internalize those voices as we grow and soon we are doing it to ourselves.

- **Things we inherit:** Even if our family or early

childhood units didn't come down on us, we may have watched a parent berating themselves for their own capabilities. Or we watched an adult struggle with depression, anxiety, or a variety of "-isms" like workaholism, alcoholism, or just plain ol' "my life is hardism." It's impossible not to take on some of what our parents do. Children are little mimicking machines and internalize the adult world around them in order to survive: we mimic how to eat, socialize, love, and be loved. We don't filter out those things that don't serve us as adults; we bring them with us. We often bring them along biologically as well. You may have genes that give you similar mental health behaviors as your relatives. Lack of self-confidence may run in your family and consequently, in you.

- **Dysfunctional environments:** Finally, we can find ourselves growing up in, or as adults, landing in situations that have dysfunction beyond what we've considered here so far. Poverty, abuse, illness, accidents, loss of family, and other trauma can all make it difficult to see ourselves in a positive light. It's hard to know your worth when you don't know where your next meal is coming from or whether you are safe in your own home. This is true especially if this is happening to us as children. Because the biology of a child demands that it make sense of the world around it in order to best survive, the conclusion we end up making is that something is "wrong" with us or else this wouldn't be happening. This belief can stay with us the rest of our lives if we don't consciously work with it as adults. Even if you had a great childhood, life can bring us unexpected setbacks that make us question our worth. It's hard to feel on top of the world if you are laid off, rejected by a spouse, or go through bankruptcy. Any major life event can set us back, at least for awhile.

- **Lack of resiliency:** Even if there are no dysfunctions happening within a family, all families are exposed to the fast-paced, stress-filled demands that modern life can make, even when things are good, like the kids participating in sports and activities and the adults having jobs they love. It's just a lot to juggle and demands that we have the capacity to reprioritize, manage stress, and bounce back when there are challenges or adversity. To create resiliency in children, the adults around them have to model handling disappointment and moving on from it. They have to create space for children to figure things out while staying connected to others. It's not always easy, as many adults did not learn these same things for themselves. Even praise can inadvertently cause us to question our capabilities. Children who are praised in ways such as "Oh, you're so smart!" or "Wow, you did that perfectly!" are much more likely to avoid challenging situations because they worry that next time they might not get it right. On the other hand, kids who are praised for their process such as "Way to go, you really stuck with that" or "How did that feel to focus on that until you got it done?" head toward taking on greater and greater challenges.[6] A child praised in their process creates resiliency as they learn that overcoming challenges leads to success. They do better than the child who is praised in a way that is outcome, or comparison to results, based.

- **Culture of comparison:** Another way that modern life can hurt our confidence is that we live in an age rife with comparison. Between binge watching Netflix, YouTube videos on everything, and social media pings letting you know what someone else is up to, you can constantly tune into how others live from what they wear, to what they do, to what they had for breakfast. It used to be only supermodels/actors in TV ads, magazines, and billboards where we saw comparative images that were damaging to our body image and to our wallets in keeping up with the Joneses. Now, we are comparing ourselves to what we perceive as other ordinary people doing it better than us. Nothing could be more damaging to authenticity than to constantly compare yourself to someone else. From a spiritual or authenticity perspective, comparison doesn't even exist as a concept. Think about it for a moment. Yes, there are traits that are different or the same when you look at two people, but it's only in the judgment of those things being better or worse that creates a problem. This creates difficulty from the mundane ways we judge our day-to-day living to even greater ones like body image issues or where we feel less than just because of our gender. Sexism comes from this comparison and judgment idea and has been with us for centuries. The notion that somehow women are inferior when compared to men, and all the resulting policies, social customs, and ways that women are treated as a result can leave even the most talented woman wondering whether she's enough.

No wonder almost all of us question our worth at some point or another! You might ask then what we can do about it. From my point of view, we must each craft a path for handling whatever our flavor of worth issue we have. Learning to accept that it arises for us and giving ourselves a way to get through it each time it does is the ultimate in self-acceptance.

Here are four steps toward creating this acceptance for yourself. Use these as a guide to create your own pathway.

1. **Assess:** you can't address it if you don't realize it's happening. We can get so habitual in our thinking and actions that we don't even notice that a feeling of worthlessness has snuck in. Step one then is to catch when you're feeling less than. Notice what your version of this feels like. Do you fall into comparison while scrolling through FB or Instagram and the next thing you know, you don't feel up to taking your next biz step? Or do you get excited about writing that new blog or updating your website and then fizzle out when you sit down to do it after thoughts of "I'll never get this right" have crept

in? By noticing your own patterns around not feeling worthy, you take an important step toward dismantling them.

2. **Admit:** now that you know you're feeling it, it's important to say it. We can all fall into the thinking that we are somehow unique in feeling unworthy. Simply not true! A big part of getting to your authenticity comes from admitting what actually is occurring rather than what you wish was. Message your friend or partner, write it in your journal, or share it a trusted business colleague. When you admit that it's happening, you take a giant step toward deflating it. You also give others permission to admit they feel it, too, which can make you feel less alone and more capable of changing it.

3. **Act:** This might be the hardest step. Even though you don't feel like you can or should take your business actions when you feel unworthy, it's important to do it anyway. Often we think that we need to "feel" better first and then we'll take that next action. But it works in the opposite way. If you feel like you might not get it right, but take the action of reaching out or writing that article or creating that class anyway, you signal to yourself that you actually are worth it. If you are highly critical of all your efforts, it's the act of doing them anyway and saying "good enough" that will decrease that critical voice. Worth and confidence are the by products of taking small steps forward, even when you are afraid. Here's the thing for everyone regarding worth and your biz—you will never do enough personal growth work to feel worthy moving forward in your business. It's the moving forward in your business that will bring up the perfect type of personal work you need to do to keep going and create your feelings of worth. It's the very act of building your business that will increase you feeling worthy, not the other way around.

4. **Assist:** In addition to taking actions within your business, it's helpful to find other ways to support you in

feeling more worthy over time. One thing I like is to create a perspective that looks at what's right, rather than what's not. A tool for this is to build a brag list. Start by listing at least 25 things you are good at. These can be small things like making great pancakes or having a nice laugh. Every day add a couple more things to your list and every day read through your list. Although it seems simple, this is a great technique for rewiring your neural circuits to look for what's right. There are so many other ways you can assist yourself in feeling an ongoing sense of worth: take on a mindfulness practice, spend time in nature, find ways of moving your body that you love, practice meeting your own needs, eat foods you love, and on and on. The goal is to consciously support yourself on a path that lets you know you're worth it. If it's a daily thing that you feel unworthy and has been with you for a long time, part of your assisting might include therapy, somatic work, tapping, or EMDR. These types of work can help you untie the tight knot your worth issues have around you and help you get moving in your business.

Questions for Reflection:

- Do you know your worth or is this an area you need to work with?
- Which of the reasons listed resonates as causing worth issues for you?
- Are you willing to craft a path toward worth for yourself?

Step Toward Your Purpose

I've talked about us real girls being purpose driven entrepreneurs throughout this book. The word *purpose* in this phrase has meant doing work that contributes to the good of others and/or to the planet. To make the world a better place. We may know some of our purpose of our work, but how many of us have actually stopped to define our own personal purpose? It can be hard to do this precisely, because most of us have a purpose that is multi-faceted. We are here to make a contribution to and learn from a variety of situations including in families, communities, passions/interests, and in the work we do. It's not often that we only have one purpose and that it's crystal clear. It's more common that we have a mix of purposes in several categories, and we have to blend these together to be well seated in a life full of purpose.

I have noticed one common theme to many people's purposes. For this, let's consider nature. When you spend time in nature, you begin to see the multitudes of patterns and tiny details that are part of every living thing. Attention to detail and design radiates from even the most minute bud. Study nature a bit and you'll see an intelligent eco-system. Every piece of our planet seems designed for a purpose. In nature, I see purpose as one of five qualities: holding, growing, being, receiving, or composting. It turns out that purpose can be an energetic thing, not just a doing thing.

Does one of these five energies resonate with you as part of your purpose? This is usually a theme that tends to run through many of your interactions, at work and at home. Try to identify the energies you belong to, and which you offer to others. Viola, you immediately see a part of your purpose. As I've discussed, mine is around growth. Quite the opposite, my husband's quality is around holding. You can see this difference in how we move through our lives, both in business and personally. I am constantly moving forward in all things, and often encouraging those around me to do the same. I'm always in action heading *toward* something and rarely hold onto anything. My husband, whose purpose is more about holding, is always carrying many situations, people, and things as they come to be. He gathers things to him, sorts them, and stays with them for long periods of time.

The one you belong to causes some struggle, as you are here to learn how to be in this energy. You will seek others who do it well, so that you can learn to do it. Others will seek you for what you do well, so that they can learn to do it, too. Hence, growing driven people may find themselves surrounded by people who are laid back and simply receive in life. The driven person is trying to learn to just be. On the other hand, the laid-back person wants to learn to grow. There is a purpose in both, and purpose in coming together.

Stepping into your larger purpose helps the evolution of our planet and to lift the vibrational frequency to a point where we transcend much of the lower or heavy vibrational experiences we currently experience. It allows us to leave behind low vibrational energies like guilt, shame, and doubt to live in the lighter states of acceptance, joy, and love. This process has been happening for years, but recently there has been a shift in the energies making it possible to speed things along exponentially. Have you noticed the change? It's sort of like shoveling snow or digging dirt. At first, it seems like each shovel full only moves a little bit. Over time, since a lot has been cleared, each scoop seems to move a lot. Soon, with only little bits left, it's easy to push it away with your boot—or even to finally clear it with one good breath.

On the work front, many entrepreneurs want to break free in their professional life to do what fulfills them, using their gifts and talents to make a difference and earning more than enough money. For some, this means letting go of overblown ideas of contribution, and focusing on where they can make a difference with what's in front of them. For others, this means stepping out of a deadening, safe, or comfortable situation to contribute their real gifts and talents. In either case, doing so will feel profoundly uncomfortable for most. Why? Because, they are being asked to grow into a state different from where they currently are.

As part of your purpose, the larger opportunity for your business sits at the edge of your consciousness, beckoning to you. Think of that activity or impact within reach for your business. It is bigger than you can imagine, farther away than you can see, and yet it still calls to you. For most, it's scary to contemplate, although, with all its energy, it can feel extremely exciting, as well.

I can think of dozens of clients who've come to me with the idea that there is something bigger calling them from within their business. Usually it's that they've been doing their work for a while and are starting to see the impact their work is really making. Perhaps they thought they were teaching clients conscious movement, but were really helping them drop old limitations and accept themselves. Or perhaps they thought they were offering them image and beauty consulting but their clients were actually learning to stand up for themselves. Possibly their business started because they took a certain kind of training, and at first, only worked with their clients in that way, but over time developed their own version of the work. Then the urge to share it in a bigger way, or make a larger contribution starts calling. The idea to speak on a larger stage, touch more lives, or create their own brand comes up in visualizations with their businesses. Usually they feel disbelief, like "Who me?" when they see this possible future. Excitement comes, too, as they contemplate how their life could change and how their work could grow. Only about a third begin to step forward toward this new reality, as the rest tuck it away as not the right time or realize that growing is not something they are up for. Those who step forward begin a journey that stretches them in ways they couldn't have guessed. Sometimes they arrive where they meant to go; other times their path veers along the way and they go somewhere else. But all look back on the ride as a journey where they grow into a bigger, better version of themselves.

The main question is whether you are up for the ride or not. If you are, you will be stretched and pushed to new places. You will feel a lot of uncertainty and being comfortable will become a distant memory. But you will also drop that achy feeling that there is something more for you to pursue. A lot of your irritation, tiredness, and numb feelings will disappear. You will feel totally, wildly alive as you live more and more in your purpose. You will realize that you have more inner capacity than you ever thought possible. You will see your courage even though you will often feel afraid. Doing this brings you into your authenticity in a fuller way. Becoming more and more aligned with your purpose is a path worth pursuing.

Finding and living your purpose lets you feel totally, wildly alive

---

How can you find yours? Chances are that the universe has been sending you hints and nudges for a while. Have you been listening? Maybe you've chosen to ignore those little prompts, or have acknowledged them, but thought they would take too much work to actually implement. Or, you have no idea how you would get from where you are to where those visions show you. Honestly, you just have to take a step forward and wait for the next one to reveal itself. I often speak with folks who are standing on the sidelines waiting for the whole picture to reveal itself before they are going to decide if they will move forward or not. It doesn't work that way. It's only when you begin to follow those inner promptings toward what you think is in alignment with your purpose that more is revealed. And over time, you get the sense of the work you are really meant to do.

To get started, you can ask yourself what you came here to do, who you came here to serve, or what contribution you want to make. If you can drop into any of these questions, you may find some clues. But these are only the beginning! Then you must start moving toward these, even in tiny steps, to move along this pathway.

Questions for Reflection:

- Do you identify with one of these purpose energies: holding, growing, being, receiving, or composting?
- Do you see how others in your life hold other energies of purpose you may need to learn?
- Does an opportunity call in your work that scares or excites you?
- Does this help you see ways you could contribute to others or the world?
- Can you see one small step you can take to head toward this new opportunity?

Be Honest and Find Your Heart's Desire

Often entrepreneurs focus on what they think they should do, such as obligations and best practices within their industry. Yes, these are important, but your objectives should also be shaped by your real desires, hopes, and your personality. Trying to market something you don't really want to do or towards goals lacking meaning can be difficult, and also doesn't get the best results. Once you have a sense of your purpose in your work, you need to take the next step and dream the ways it might come to be in the world.

How do you find your authentic desires *and* keep them

realistic? Your state of mind matters here. You cannot dream into being that which you cannot imagine, nor that which you feel you don't deserve. It can also be difficult to dream when you are tired, cranky, or feeling low. In those moments, you need to wait until you are in a better state so that you can daydream, imagine, and think expansively.

It's easy to scale dreams back, but it's difficult to paint them larger when they start off small. Therefore, go big in your thinking. Are you helping others make a difference in their lives? Are you making the world a better place in some way? Are you creating a career that helps you express yourself in a profound way? Or are you doing all three? Follow your contribution all the way out to its greatest impact. Fill yourself with the possibilities for a different kind of world and your place within it.

Often, we think small because we are afraid our big dream may be out of reach or, worse, that we don't deserve it. Thinking this way overrides divine intelligence and the notion that we are created with a purpose. Who are you to question whether you should take this opportunity, or keep yourself safe, rather than stretch to your full potential?

Some would say it's a sin to ignore the opportunities before you. At best, it may be your ego—or some version of temptation—to ignore your growth possibilities in favor of feeling safe or secure in material things. Even though virtually every spirituality and religion says to ignore the material in favor of the spiritual, this concept proves difficult for the Western mind. We are afraid of what we'll have to give up or the disruption we'll feel if we move toward our highest goal.

Remember, you are only dreaming at this point. This can help you around the fear. All journeys take a thousand steps to accomplish. You'll only ever be asked to take the next step—not all the steps at once. This way, your risk stays quite small.

You can tell yourself it's all on paper at this point, and you don't have to start if you don't want to! Our fears sometimes need to be coddled and held to quiet down enough for us to move forward.

Once you have your larger dreams identified, celebrate! Then, move through rest of this book to learn how to bring them to be. This will ensure you are bringing in the practical means to enact your dreams. I've noticed a lot of purpose-driven entrepreneurs carry around their dreams, as if writing them in their journal will bring them to fruition. In truth, you need to follow sound guidance and take practical actions to accomplish them.

Create Authentic Goals

Now that you have your larger dream identified, you must combine that with your goals for your business to lead you there. Do you have written objectives for where you are headed? Do you even know how you would identify them?

Your business goals should be specific and measurable, both so that you can reach them and know when you've gotten there. They are usually about the money you'd like to earn, the impact you'd like to make, and the development of products/services you need to do.

How does that relate to your big dreams? Your desires are usually end-of-the-line items, such as being a published author, having a thriving business, or traveling the world doing your work. Imagine a staircase and your big dream sits at the top of the stairs. Your authentic objectives are the steps you're going to walk up to arrive at your dream. No one I know can stand at the bottom of the stairs and wish themselves to the top. You must make the effort to put one foot in front of the other and climb each step to get there. The upward steps are stages you must go through on your way, as your big dream may take years to accomplish. It could be two years away, five years away, or even more than 10 years. Each year, you'll have goals or objectives you need to reach to end up at that big dream someday.

For example, let's say your big dream is to have a small firm offering graphic design to clients around the country. Imagine this as the big goal at the top of the staircase. Let's look now from the bottom, leading up to this top point. Year one—or step one—you'll need to create your marketing materials such as a website, business card, and LinkedIn profile. You'll also need to find ways to become visible to potential clients through networking, or creating an online presence. And, you'll need to start landing jobs and executing them flawlessly.

Your objectives/goals for this first year might be written on your plan like this:

1. Create initial marketing materials (website, business card, online profiles)
2. Sign up and attend six networking groups in the first three months; attend two regularly for the rest of year.
3. Gain $3,000 in new business monthly for first three months; increase to $5,000 monthly for the rest of the year.

Those three goals will likely take you all your first year to reach, maybe more. They only support you; they are not enough to have a thriving small firm. So, you must keep going up the stairs.

Years two and three will be to continue with year one's goals, removing goal one's start-up materials—though they will need regular updates—and adding the creation of systems for finances, marketing, and client servicing. You don't want to spend your time always doing the mundane things like balancing your books, paying invoices, creating client contracts, and answering emails. You want to create systems to handle routine things more quickly or automatically, so that you have time to pursue new business. To keep business coming in, you might look to increase your visibility in your networking groups by taking on a volunteer position within the group, or taking on other kinds of new visibility. Finally, you look for ways to increase earnings enough to pay for staff beginning the next year, so that you can meet that goal of being a firm, not a solopreneur.

Year's two and three list might look like this:

1. Develop systems for ongoing finance management, marketing, and client servicing (describe each specifically with detail. For example, upgrade to QuickBooks, create auto scheduled monthly newsletter, and implement online contract signing for clients).
2. Increase visibility within networking group, or create a new visibility avenue that creates 20 new leads per month.
3. Identify and create a strategy for pursuing new revenue streams or increase earnings by 30%.

Years four and five will have new goals meant to increase the types of jobs you are awarded, and the systems needed to support staff. Can you see how it might take five years before you have enough regular business and the base for your business to have staff? That might be only your first employee.

Of course, this holds if you are starting from scratch. Many people spin off of an existing job or skill set when starting a new business. In this example, if you were already doing graphic design for a company, you might spin off to your own business with a couple of good clients and hire a staff person right away. But, you'll still have those other objectives to meet over time, so that you can expand. No matter where you start, you must break down your big dream into goals for the coming year, and then, break each of those goals down into monthly actions.

I prefer to call them objectives, rather than goals, for two reasons. First, the word goal can be uncomfortable for purpose-driven entrepreneurs. It's too corporate, too competitive, and too linear. Second, it's a good reminder to be objective, not emotional, about where you want to go. Sure, it's good to bring some emotion in, like how good it could feel to reach them, but you also must have some practical and actionable ideas about where you're going. You don't want to invite in the more negative type emotions like fear, doubt, and worry, as these usually block us.

Download a staircase worksheet at lindabasso.com/authenticmarketer

4

FIND YOUR TRUTH

The Truth About Truth

It's easy to look at truth as a black-and-white concept—true or not true. However, we repeatedly see, even in science, truth often changes. New evidence comes to light disproving a previously proved theory, for example. Facts and statistics can be interpreted to mean one thing—or another. New advancements could change our current understanding. Lucky for us, because this is the very thing that lets us each be different, yet authentic.

We live in a dynamic changing environment where scientific experiments don't always produce repeatable results. Every few years, we hear of former theories proven untrue when new evidence came to light. It's safe to drink coffee; no, it isn't. Babies need to lie on their side to avoid sudden infant death syndrome, or is it their back? Experts with excellent credentials find they are at odds with other experts who have equally impressive credentials. Some experiments have even proven the outcome depends on the scientist observing it. This suggests science may only be a snapshot of what we currently believe true in the physical realm.

Things get even more fluid when you add in that truth seems to be deeply personal. We often say—and experience—that what's true for one person holds false for another. In this light, the idea of a mass culture seems ludicrous. It all depends on what's authentic for you. Take diets, for example. For some, eating only slow-cooked meats and vegetables will maintain health. Others swear by raw foods with no animal proteins. Some thrive on low-fat, high-carb diets, while others do just the opposite. I can find a Ph.D. level doctor who has done the research to back up each of these diets, yet one set of evidence contradicts the other.

Pick up a book at the bookstore and look next to it for a book proving the opposite. The same is true for medicine. Yesterday's miracle cure doesn't prove out over time. One patient will have a predictable response to a given medication, while another doesn't. Stress washes over each of us individually, causing some to become ill, while others are energized.

Though we all long for things to be black-and-white to ease our way, life doesn't seem to support this all-or-nothing approach. Instead, we face complexity, unknowns, and many shades of gray as we live along the spectrum between black and white.

From a spiritual perspective, here's the truth about truth. It ranges over time and space to encompass all that is. A situation and its opposite are both true. Depending on the situation, circumstances, and people involved, it plays out in one way now and possibly another in the future. Spiritually, this duality has always been tolerated as what makes the universe whole. We are all good and evil, selfish and generous, honest and dishonest. Sure, it can be about the degree to which we are each, but both are true. They may be considered two representations of a single underlying reality, the underlying reality of non-duality.

Even in science, we begin to see the truth in contradictions. The theories of general relativity and quantum fields are incompatible theories of reality, yet both prove true on their own scale. Things we think are solid, like furniture, are made of moving particles. Black holes draw everything inward, but somehow simultaneously emit radiation out. Rather than being linear, time, it turns out, is a logical progression that speeds up or slows down depending on the frames of reference of who's observing. Light can be both a wave and a particle, showing that something can indeed be in two places at once. Even the animal kingdom weighs in with the contrarian platypus—which contains genes that match mammal, reptile, and bird.

As you can see, contradictions are not as problematic as you may initially think. Universally, black-and-white thinking almost never works.

The same holds true for marketing.

Clients come to me sure their marketing is right or wrong. They believe there must be one way to do something and if they could just find it, their business would work better than it does. Truth be told, for any one business, there are many ways of doing the marketing, not just one. That's why we can each find our authentic way. And which will succeed? That's the magic question and can only be answered through experimentation to find what works for now. We then must look for a new way when that stops working. In the end, there's no black-and-white answer. Rather, it's all an ongoing process.

Successful marketing depends on experimentation and

responding to what's happening in your market. There is no one formula or approach that works for everyone, every time. Rather, you must be willing to try, try, and try again to find the things that bring in clients. And be willing to shift it as soon as it no longer works. Marketing is organic in this way as it is ever-shifting and much more an art than a science. This can be a relief as it frees you up to be much less serious and rigid in your marketing.

Other clients become stressed out because they think the only way to be successful in their marketing means doing things they don't like to do. Again, marketing success is relative. There is no one way to do it, only your unique way. You can hate social media and still find an effective way to use it in your business marketing—or not do it at all. Or you can hate networking and still be visible enough to garner the confidence of people you meet. And, yes, even introverts can succeed in getting in front of enough potential clients. We need to step out of the exclusionary thinking of "or" (i.e.) you can be an introvert *or* you can meet enough people for a thriving business, but not both. Instead, consider how someone may be an introvert *and* can still have connective conversations given the right circumstances. Or consider that someone can hate social media *and* guide their business into the online world in ways that fit. Similarly, you can set up a business that fits your personal rhythms *and* earn enough money. In the end, success can usually be found in finding the *and*, not staying with the *or*.

What's True for You?

As we discussed earlier, honesty is an important part of authentic marketing. But there is some additional truth telling needed for your marketing to be successful. These truths are more subtle and can sometime be hard to discern. Yet, they form the basis of powerful visibility that draws clients toward you.

One part is to know what's true for yourself as you move through life.

Finding your truth is powerful. Yet, we avoid looking afraid of what we will discover. The truth doesn't have to scare, nor ask you to make painful changes. It always sets you free. Your truth fills you with incredible joy as it fills you up with your very nature. Truth has a very high vibration, not bound with inconsistencies or lower emotions like guilt or blame. Your truth does not depend on what others would like for you, nor does it depend on their fears for you.

You must find your truth in order to do your marketing well. Finding yours helps to create the alignment needed for effective marketing that we discussed in earlier chapters. The more alignment you have in the work you do, who you do it for, how you do it, and the role it plays in your overall life, the easier it is for you to share about it and for the right people to find you. This is really at the heart of your authenticity! Deep alignment makes it easy to share yourself with others. You rarely feel like an imposter and if you do, it's easier to shake off and come back to your knowing your own worth. Your alignment makes it easier to find your unique way rather than following every trend or random piece of advice. It's like you have a compass for knowing which way to head. When you lack this alignment, you may find yourself pulled in many directions and lack the focus to pull off powerful visibility. This won't draw clients in. It's as if they can sense something is amiss and though they cannot name it, they just won't choose you.

Truth, a subtle and delicate thing, must come through experience, not intellect. You were created to have this experience. That is why it comes often through spirituality, transformational growth, or physical movement. Recognizing the truth helps you live in congruence with your purpose. When you are cut off from your truth, a part of yourself shuts down, which is very painful. That's what you should be scared of—not the truth itself!

You find it by learning to pay close attention to your inner promptings, desires, urges, and inklings. Difficult? No. Subtle? Yes.

To find your truth you must become sensitive to your response to the things that come along in your life. You will feel a strong resonance in the presence of your truth or sometimes a strong conflict. Neutrality means that it doesn't hold much for you. If you feel a deep pull toward something, give yourself the option to pursue it until you know the truth of it for yourself. Likewise, if you are in deep conflict about something and you give the conflict enough attention, an informative bit of truth will emerge. Searching for these threads of truth takes your entire lifetime. So if you've felt pressure to get there soon, relax. Stick with what's true for you currently. The remaining truths in your life are making their way toward you. Sometimes, you can't know the complete truth yet, as pieces of it are still in process. Your maturity level and life experience play a big part in accessing your truths.

Finding and living your truths contribute to what you came here to do. It adds to the overall collective knowledge of our experience here. It can get complicated because our truths are often obscured or covered by others' hopes and fears for us. Or we may have had negative reactions to our truth when we were young. It can be scary to step into our truth if we think we will lose love or connection with others because of it.

Fortunately, it's not important to understand every detail of a truth. Instead, know that seeking and living the truth to the best of your understanding meets your highest purpose;

which is to say, living your truth is what you came here to do. You are unique and have different abilities, intellect, emotional systems, etc., so of course, your understanding of truth will be different from someone else's. More importantly, search for *yours*, and sit in the knowledge you are living a very high calling.

Finding and living your truth to the best of your ability is your highest purpose

---

Another part is sharing your unique point of view.

It turns out that being truthful in your marketing materials serves you well by not merely telling the truth about your services or product, but your unique truths as well. This is why there can be 20 different real estate professionals in the same area and all are getting business. Or why you find yourself drawn to work with one coach but not another. It's not fancy marketing language that creates this reaction. It's their personal take on their business, how they see the world, and what contribution they want to make to others that draws you toward them.

Although this may seem hard to figure out for yourself, it's not. You've likely been thinking about your business and clients through this lens since the beginning. You just may have not articulated it in your marketing materials yet. This could be a major reason you don't have as much business as you'd like, or are drawing in the wrong clients. Let's look at an example to illustrate.

Annie is a health and fitness coach. When she starts her business, she talks about the need to get healthy and shares information on her website about eating well, working out, and other tools she can use to help you in your health journey. She shares articles she finds about being healthy on her website that talk about health for men, women, and families. When she lists how she can help you, it ranges from eating healthy, to all the different types of workouts you can do, to the differences in several popular diets. Her list of services includes tailored fitness plans, personal training, motivation & support, and nutritional guidance. She gets a few clients here and there but she is struggling to fill her practice.

Lauren, on the other hand, has taken some time to look at her field of health and wellness and think about how she is the same as other trainers, as well as how she is different. She comes to see that although she wants people to be healthy, she does not personally agree with the idea of dieting or restricting foods in order to create a certain type of body shape. It bothers her personally that her field puts such a heavy emphasis on how people look rather than on how they feel or how they rate in health metrics that are not appearance based. She sees that a particular group that struggles with this is women whose children are young and are experiencing their bodies changing from having children, getting older, and not having time to workout like they used to. Plus, they tend to stress eat or just not have time for healthy cooking even though they long to feed their families well.

Lauren had a similar experience 5 years ago when her children were 2 & 4 years old. In her marketing materials, she shares her point of view that health in women is about more than how we look. She shares tips and ideas for women to manage a family, work, and health in emotionally healthy ways. She shares her personal story about her struggles during that time of her life and what she did to overcome them. The services she offers are specific to solving the problems these women face: private training with childcare, online short workouts they can do with children, food plans that include *recipes & shopping lists and can be prepared in under 30 minutes, teaching mindfulness techniques that create greater self-acceptance. Not only is her private practice full, but Lauren is getting requests from women in other states and is making her online materials available to women around the country.*

Can you see how differently these two business owners are sharing? Annie is sharing generically about her field, Lauren is sharing her unique point of view. It would be easy to pass by Annie's messaging of "being healthy". It just isn't that inspiring for any of us (even though it should be!) But if you are a mother, Lauren's messaging would feel compelling to you and like she really cares about you and your journey. That is the crux of sharing your truths: it's not really about you, it's about caring so much for your ideal clients that you want to meet them where they are. Can you imagine trying to start a relationship in your personal life by being generic? Can you imagine saying "Hi, I like everybody and to do anything" and expect to find friends? Nope. You would share the unique things that light you up and matter to you in hopes of finding similar folks to share time with. In your marketing, it is the same. Sharing your unique truths is a powerful tool to use to draw in exactly the right kind of client and enough of them.

What Is Too Much Truth?

Earlier we talked about transparency and how to let more of you come out in the name of authenticity. Clients want to know the real deal when it comes to the people and companies they buy from. We touched on the question "How transparent should you be?" but now let's dig a little deeper.

It's one thing for a celebrity or the founder of a once-small but now ginormous company (think Apple or Zappos) to have their philosophy and personal life splashed around.

It's OK because they made it. The coolness of their success overshadows any potential backlash about their beliefs, approach, or path there. The public can be radically accepting of a wide range of beliefs when success is involved. But when is sharing your truth too much? The answer is a little tricky until you reframe it. When you ask that question what you are wondering is when is sharing your truth going to lead to a negative response from others.

First, consider exactly what does too much mean? We've all heard of over sharing or the phrase TMI (too much information). We aren't exactly sure when transparency in our beliefs moves to overwhelming the other person and hindering rather than fostering a good connection. This, like all of marketing, requires that you put on the hat of the other person in order to find an answer.

Sharing works best when you've considered both how and what you want to share and combine that with what will create harmony and connection where you are sharing it. This applies to random social media comments to sharing your personal background to full on rants about what's not working in the world. You are always a representative of your business whether you work for yourself or a company. In other words, all of your opinions and ideas represent who you are as a person and that whole person is going to be reacted to by others.

Am I saying to keep your personal opinions to yourself? Not at all. I'm saying that you have to be conscious with them, and if you own a business, keep them in alignment with your brand. If you have a deeply held belief about animal cruelty, and you are in a conservative industry like finance, it's probably not your best bet to publish photos of horrific animal cruelty depictions on your social media. But if you host a high-end fundraiser for the Humane Society, you will get accolades and be authentic at the same time.

Want to call attention to something that is a heated topic in your personal life? Consider sharing an article by someone and asking for feedback from others on their thoughts instead of sharing only your own hot opinion. Or share your thoughts in a blog post that explains how you are wrestling with this personal idea and how it's impacting your business. We've all read articles and posts or heard talks that deal with difficult material that are done well. Study these examples, take note of what works in them and what you want to emulate for yourself. We've also all seen instances where the share is uncomfortable or feels unclean or attacking. Study these as well so you know what you *don't* want to do.

If you have an opinion that is not popular, consider why you are sharing it. Maybe you are meant to call attention to an issue or be the guide for others who have a similar opinion. But get clear and be as sensitive as you can in how you share it with an idea of how you can add to or shape the discussion in a way that moves the issue along. Just like any communication, you have to consider whom it's meant for and what would be well received by them or inspire them to act. It's back to our earlier discussion in transparency about the idea of appropriate and capable of existing together in harmony. If your communication only causes people to feel uncomfortable or poked at, they are likely to push back. If you are constantly venting or ranting, you are likely to offend rather than invite potential clients even if your brand is one that is slightly irreverent. It's about blending your need for self-expression with how you want to be received by the world around you.

What if you're not famous or wildly successful and you come with a background littered with difficulty? What if your past has made you stronger, shaped who you are, and why you do the work you do—but isn't rosy and easy to explain? I've faced this and worked with many clients who face it, too. I call us survivorpreneurs because we are small business owners who've gone through some tough stuff and made it anyway. Ultimately, I want us to move past surviving to thriving.

When you share your truth, you're being brave, bold, and beautiful in your business

---

In claiming our truths, and making them transparent to others, we take an important step toward becoming bold, beautiful, and brave in our businesses. Yes, there are ways to share your story without over-sharing. You can be transparent about the dysfunction, stress, abuse—or the illness, accident, or mistake—that shaped the entrepreneur you've become. To be clear, I'm not talking about whitewashing any violent belief or disrespect of others. I am saying you can bring all of you to your business and message in a way that brings you clients, rather than drives people away. Let go of the fear that if you share the real you, no one will want to work with you. You can stop using the mask of what you think you are supposed to be and hoping it works, which, sadly, it rarely does.

Instead be brave and admit the ways you've struggled. How your journey, warts and all, has brought you here. Especially in your biography—or about section—of your marketing materials. It will feel weird and ungraceful at first. That's because most of us were taught not to share socially unpleasant topics. Remember the adage that if you don't have something nice to say, don't say anything? Let me assure you that it's nice to share yourself with potential clients, so that they can make a good decision for themselves about whom to work with. It's not nice to pretend to be something you're not, or to hold back part of yourself in shame.

How?

First, get the details out for yourself and feel whatever feelings they bring up. Then, meet with a copywriter/editor/messaging type person who's got an empathetic ear and the savvy to shape that into something clients can relate to. Often we are not the best person to see how our story might inspire others or make them feel connected to us as humans. Going it alone in this brings up more of the earlier trauma and feeling that you don't have the support you need. So get help for this step. Seek and you will find a way to message your difficult truth in ways that are safe and supportive.

When Your Truth Aligns With the Spiritual

What if your truth and your unique point of view are spiritual? It can be hard to know how to express this well, or if you should express it at all. As with any messaging question, the answer is that it depends. First, look at your business and see if it's an obvious fit. If your business is religious or spiritual in some way, or your ideal clients are religious or spiritual, then it makes sense to bring this into your messaging. Examples could be therapists or coaches who focus on Christian (or other religious) clients, or healers who deal with energetic & spiritual ideas in their work. I believe these businesses should profess their point of view in their messaging. It could be in your business name, or your tagline for example, as in "supporting Christian couples through the covenant of marriage" or something else that gets right at the heart of how or who you serve. If you use energetic, spiritual, or religious tools regularly in your business to get your clients their results, then you should include this to some degree in your messaging so that your marketing messages are in alignment with what your business does.

It could break trust if you don't. I can imagine a healer who served clients from a Buddhist point of view that didn't indicate that in their marketing materials and the confusion that might cause when someone inquired about their services and started hearing Zen based terminology. In a time where people are looking for transparency, it's a break in the experience people have of your business and how it acts when there is a lack of alignment between how you put your business out there and how your business is experienced by the user. Especially if your business creates some kind of community around it, it's important that you are direct about your underlying beliefs. The idea is to create as much transparency as needed for clients to make a good, informed decision for themselves.

I remember going to a conference once where all the materials leading up to the conference were about business and becoming an author. Imagine my surprise when at the beginning of the two day meeting that the 400+ people around me joined hands in prayer before we started! Although I have nothing against prayer and even do it in my own life, it was the beginning of the end with that group and me as I came to see many small ways that their messaging and their values were not in alignment. They constantly said they were secular, but often brought up biblical passages or prayer in their meetings. They said they were welcoming to all points of view but often had religious speakers who had definite roles for people. There were even sometimes disparaging remarks made from the community about other cultures. As much as they wanted to be inclusive, they weren't there yet and their marketing wasn't honest about the type of clients they typically served. If I had known they served a primarily Christian audience, those behaviors would not have caught me off guard. I could have chosen whether I felt up to immersing myself in that culture rather than feeling surprised by it.

Some businesses are mixed and could go either way. If you are in the wedding industry for example, it's up to you whether you are going to take a spiritual or secular point of view. Just decide consciously and be consistent in your messaging. If you're not sure, play with different types of messages that range from secular to spiritual to see which resonate the best for you or bring in the types of clients that are a good fit for your personality and the way you like to work. This is definitely an area where you'll want to experiment until you find the way that feels best to you, your business, and your clients. After all, you want to end up in an authentic place.

If you are in a business that tends to be secular like business or financial consulting, health or fashion, or a shopkeeper for non-religious items, you have to ask yourself why you want to share your spiritual point of view. If it's that your personal religion/spirituality is so important to you that you feel you must share it, then do so consistently. Consider the above option where you actually serve clients who share your point of view. Make sure you include messages in your marketing and the way that you share stories and examples that make your beliefs clear. In your About section or bio, consider sharing some of why your spiritual side is important to you. It's important that you share from the perspective of what's important about it to you, rather than from why others should have a similar point of view or how they should conduct themselves. You want to be honest, not preachy or missionary in your approach. Business is not place for converting others; it's a place to be your honest self so that others can make an informed choice for themselves.

Stepping out to share our spiritual beliefs can have a layer of added difficulty. Many stopped sharing our unique beliefs because we believed we would be passed over because of it. For years, we've lived under separation of church and state. I respect this principle, maintaining the right for all to choose their way of worship. At the same time, taken to the extreme, it has made our workplaces virtually devoid of spiritual practices—and, too often, principles. Add to that our scientific age doesn't take seriously that which can't be proven, and the workplace has suffered with too little compassion, justice, and love.

There was a time in history when expressing your spiritual views could mean not just passing over, but persecution. We all grew up learning about the Spanish Inquisition, the Holocaust, and the Irish Republican Army (IRA). These are gruesome truths for young minds to comprehend. What we missed in that history lesson was the fact that the violence was rarely over heartfelt beliefs, but rather, over fervor and favor. The extreme acts all came from someone whose beliefs were radical and extremist, rather than following the spirit of the religion. Or they didn't come from spiritual beliefs at all, but rather the political power tied to the situation. Today's news? Not so different.

Spirituality and religion have also provided comfort, wisdom, and good advice to millions of folks for hundreds of years. Couldn't it be that similar to human beings, these traditions have some good and some bad? We wouldn't execute a person for having some flaws, and I don't believe we should completely walk away from these traditions either.

Find the traditions and practices that resonate with you. Step beyond how your family practiced. Explore other traditions—like those in the last chapter—to find the one or ones that work for you. If it's not in a formal tradition, find the separate pieces and parts that come together to make your approach whole for you. If it's nature, so be it. If it's a church, fine. If it's just a belief in something greater, go with that. You need to embrace your beliefs and feel peaceful inside about them. If you are in a certain religion, but feel inner conflict and doubt and are not actively engaged in working that out for yourself, you are not gaining the benefit of having that spiritual practice in your life.

You must *be* the beliefs you have, not simply broadcast them. The oak tree doesn't try to be anything other than what it is. We are the only species that spends time hiding itself from itself and others. Animals only do this under great duress and/or abuse. Finding the tradition or set of practices you want to partake in comes first. Creating peace and acceptance within yourself comes second. Working out whatever inner contradictions you have to create inner peace smooths the way for you to embody the beliefs.

Finding the way to share that publicly comes as the third, and oh-so-vital next step. If you find this difficult, follow the example of Pope Francis or the Dali Lama in being kind to others, yet living within your own religion and what you believe it asks of you. The quest to live your own faith deeply, while having as much tolerance and love for others, can be powerful.

Questions for Reflection:

- Do you share your values and beliefs in your marketing materials?
- Does your personal truth contain spiritual or religious beliefs? If so, do you share some version of those in your marketing?
- Can you see how difficulties and hardships in your life have shaped who you are?
- Could you be willing to share some of those difficulties and be more transparent about yourself in your business?

Your Why and How to Find It

Your beliefs about the world and how it can be improved

fuel your why. Passion, desire, and deep conviction come from this place. Every small boat sailing on big waters has a keel to keep it upright. Your why acts in the same way. No matter how you are tossed about or acted on by the forces around you, you cannot be knocked over when guided by your deeply held principles.

Your why is another way people can tell if they resonate with you and the work you do. As you know, there is no shortage of people who do what you do. If you call yourself an accountant, so do hundreds, if not thousands more. Ditto for therapists, massage therapists, copywriters, and just about every service position you can name. Products are no different. Sure, your widget might be unique in some ways, but chances are, it fills a need in someone's life that could easily be filled by another product.

I don't say this to be discouraging in any way. It's simply the truth. There's a silver lining: no one does what you do for the same reason as you, or in the same way as you. Because of this, you can touch a group of people in the world that can hear your message better than anyone else's. They resonate with what you put out, and you resonate with their needs. Articulating your why in your marketing materials creates the bridge between you and them.

No one does what you do in the same way that you do

We need our why for inspiration. This is true for our day-to-day lives as well as when the going gets tough. And it must work for people. Consider Simon Sinek and his groundbreaking work on finding your why. His TED talk on finding your why has over 30 million views, and ranks as the third most watched TED talk ever. Maybe that's due, in part, because our brains are wired for why. Ask any parent who listens to his toddler ask that question a hundred times a day. Our human fascination with story relates to why. Stories often come about because of that question and, ironically, answer it, as well.

The mind so fixates on why that sometimes it can become an obsessive loop. We've all had experiences of using the question of "why" to bemoan negative things that have happened to us. Why did this collaboration go sour? Why did they hire someone other than me? Why does updating my website seem so hard to get right?

Often one of the first steps in a self-growth program is to stop the focus on why something happened, as this tends to keep us stuck in situations as a victim. When our marketing efforts don't go the way we plan, we often fall into this why trap. Much of my work in the beginning with a new client is getting them to let go of this old story of blame and labeling.

To truly move through something, you must get past your initial urge to look for why it happened and process the situation and all the learning it has for you. For some, this means honoring the five stages of grief for full expression of their real feelings. For others, it's an active time of seeking spiritual answers or other tools such as therapy or self-inquiry work. You don't want to get stuck in looking for the why when it has to do with blame.

At best, why something happened starts as only a thought or opinion that, when held firmly, becomes a conviction. In other words, whatever story you latch onto for why something happened becomes the basis for your belief. In that capacity, why wields great power. Your convictions and beliefs—positive and negative—become the basis for how your life unfolds. You can limit yourself with these, or empower yourself.

Good news—your mind loves a task. Although seeking

why something happened is potentially a negative path, use this tenacity of the mind and turn it around. Set it to the task of enacting your why, versus asking why.

> Irene runs a well-attended dance studio and produces events for companies. She also runs a bilingual preschool and is a parent herself. She's busy and successful. But when she came to me, she didn't feel her success. She felt like giving it all up. It turns out she was exhausting herself with an internal answer she created to why her childhood had been so difficult. Early in her life, she had decided inside herself that no matter what she did, it wasn't going to make a difference. So even though she was creating success in her life now, she couldn't see it. All her activities were just ways she was trying to finally prove that she could make a difference.
>
> In our work together, she had to confront this old story. She realized that it was true that in her childhood she really wasn't able to make much of a difference. She had to grieve how awful that was for her at that time.

After releasing a lot of the emotion around the story, she also could see that not being able to make a difference was no longer true. It didn't happen instantly as she had to process a lot and change things in her world that had been built on "proving" this premise so early in her life. Finding her authentic self meant leaving her marriage and rearranging her priorities. Today she is living an entirely different life. She's identified her why as making as big of a difference as she can make in her world. Now she can see that she is doing just that in each of her endeavors. Her dance studio is teaching dozens of people confidence through movement. Her events create community and fun for hundreds more. And her preschool is touching the lives of many children and their families. Instead of giving it all up, Irene is living her why by looking at how she can increase the impact of each of these endeavors.

Why don't we all know this oh-so-important personal why? One reason comes from living in a culture that stresses collective beliefs. Our media doesn't reflect the vast array of human approaches but rather, a select one. The arts aren't celebrated as a part of our cultural expression, but rather, something to be consumed by those who can afford it. Schools aren't set up to elicit the individual thinking of each child. Children are still taught standard truths about grammar, mathematics, and worldview in a school system first developed during the Middle Ages, and systematized during the Renaissance. In other words, we've been teaching the same standardized subject matter to each generation for four hundred years.

Add to that the fact that we live in an age in which modern capitalistic approaches to living, vastly outweigh indigenous or other approaches. Very few cultures celebrate individuals finding and expressing who they really are, such as coming-of-age rituals. The few who do, mostly celebrate it as a big party like a bar mitzvah or quinceañera, rather than a plan for growth. In modern life, we are not sent on a path of individualism, but rather are asked to buy into a collective approach. Nevertheless, a spark remains in each of us. Despite the conditioning leading us to draw similar conclusions, many still have a gnawing feeling at some point to bring to light that which they alone feel the call to express in this world. Becoming aware of this inner impulse and following it can lead you to your why.

Luckily, you may already be enacting some of your why, even if you aren't fully aware of it. Since it lives inside of you, it can push you to make certain decisions, gain specific skills, and even start your specific business, even if you can't exactly name it. You may just seem drawn toward certain actions. The universe, in turn, helps you by bringing you experiences and opportunities that resonate with this inner truth. It's common when I help someone find their why that they recognize that it's been at play in their lives all along.

Finding the why of your whole life can take a lifetime. Finding your business why can be simpler. I remember finding my why through a process provided when I was receiving my certification in a Higher Ground Leadership® course using the book *The Spark, The Flame, and The Torch* by Lance Secretan. Articulating my why was startling at first, but it did shape the current version of my business. I'm grateful, because it was a pivotal time for me, and I needed some kind of keel to shape my course. Realizing my why helped me make decisions throughout that transition. Over time, I've come to see that my why has always been a part of me. I'd just never said it out loud in such a concise way before. There's no shortage of types of work in the world to help you find your why. Read Simon Sinek's work or follow the same path I did, and use Lance Secretan's book. Or here's a simple exercise to get you started.

1. Think of your business and what it does for people, or animals, or the environment. Answer this question: why is it important this gets done? For example, if you style hair, your answer might be that it's important so that people look their best. Or, if you repair cars, you might respond that it's important because it gets people where they need to go.

2. Using your answer, ask yourself why that's important. Why is it important for people to look their best or to get where they need to go? You might say that it's important that people look their best so that they feel confident about going about their lives. Use this answer and ask yourself why this is important.

3. Keep going by asking each time why it's important that your answer happen, always using your last answer as the

new subject of "why is it important?" until you've drilled down to some essence that feels meaningful to you.

Here's an example:

I fix cars for people. *Why is that important?* It gets them where they need to go. *Why is that important?* So that they can meet their obligations. *Why is that important?* So that they can take care of their families. *Why is that important?* Because strong families make life better. *Why is that important?* A better life for each person means a better world. This person's why has to do with making life better one person at a time.

Another person might answer completely differently and get to a different why:

I fix cars for people. *Why is that important?* So that they can go where they want. *Why is that important?* Getting what you want can make you happy. *Why is that important?* Happy people are nicer to be around. *Why is that important?* Well, maybe we'd have less conflict if people were happy. *Why is that important?* Less conflict might mean more peace. *Why is that important?* More peace makes the world safer. *Why is that important?* Then, I wouldn't worry about my grandchildren's future. This person's why has to do with creating happiness for a safer world.

Let whatever comes be good enough. There's no right or wrong. Remember, this starts the exploration into possibility, and this may just be the beginning of your own exploration. In my case, my why boiled down to nurturing others' growth, which is truly the keel for everything in my life. You could see this everywhere in my personal life, in my relationship with others and in my parenting. But I hadn't been expressing those things in my business copy. Now I am, and things are much clearer for potential clients as they can see that working with me will mean focusing on their growth, both personally and professionally. This is great for me because I rarely get the "wrong" kind of client coming to me anymore. The people who hire me all want this kind of growth and those who don't find another marketing consultant to work with.

Questions for Reflection:

- Did you get to any essence of your why?
- Do you see examples of this concept in your business or personal life? Give some examples.
- If your why was in the world more, how would the world be better?
- Is there anything else you can think of that's special about your why?
- Can you imagine sharing your why in your marketing materials?

What You Really Sell

Purpose-driven entrepreneurs don't go into business only to make money. Even the folks who say that money is their goal are usually trying to create something else for themselves, like freedom or the ability to choose, but that's another story.

Purpose-driven entrepreneurs often go into business to make a difference in other people's lives by contributing their skills and talents and getting paid for it. They yearn for an alignment of themselves and their work. They want to make the world a better place. That may sound like a greeting card, but times are shifting so that people believe they *can* affect change, even in some small way, to positively affect the world. Hope starts to replace cynicism. The idealism of the 60s birthed a generation that would grow up loving introspection and self-healing. And, generally, folks who've walked a self-healing path want to give back in some way. Moving to wholeness naturally leads to looking outward to see what you can contribute.

The issue seems to be money. If one could simply contribute to the world and money would somehow appear, there would be a whole lot of happy purpose-driven people out there. In truth, it can be that simple, but in our minds, there's a whole lot of complexity around money. Many of us grew up thinking that money was linked to evil—if not to the Devil himself—and to corporations, and all the wrong they do.

In truth, though, money acts as an exchange. Inherently, money connects to neither anything good or bad. The issue comes from us having set up a world where money doesn't just exchange goods, but also connects to the ability to choose, having power over others, and how resources are divided. Money as a truly neutral exchange would work only in a society in which basic dignities were respected, and the environment was considered sacred.

Instead, we are in our society with built-in barriers to the access of money. The medium you use to exchange goods cannot also be the measurement used to judge worth, ethics, and justice. In addition, because we also use money to exchange access to life-sustaining food, water, and even access to quality air, money has become entangled with survival. This gives money all kinds of energetic connotations it's not meant to have.

Entrepreneurs face a couple of ways they have to deal with this money issue. First, the notion of selling ourselves, partially because we are the person providing the service, or because the product we sell was created by us. Fascinating, because when you buy a service or product from someone, you don't believe you are buying the other person, but rather, you are paying them to provide you with a service or product. But turn it around, and it feels personal. As entrepreneurs, we should understand the truth of what we sell is not *us*.

The second issue revolves around the fact that most of us

cling to a myriad of limiting beliefs around money. Because we are in business for ourselves, we bring those beliefs into our businesses. If you work for a company, you may have these same limiting beliefs (that affect how much you earn, how much debt you create, and so on), but for the most part, the work comes in, you complete it, and get reimbursed every two weeks with a paycheck. However, when you are in business for yourself and have limiting beliefs around money, you do things like not finding enough clients, making poor business financial choices and often, either not getting your business off the ground or never earning enough from it to be considered a sustainable (let alone a thriving) business. You need to clear out your limiting beliefs so that they don't get tangled up with what you sell.

Limiting beliefs around money will show up in how much business you allow yourself to receive.

Beyond our limiting beliefs around money, we do have the desire to support others and to be supported financially for doing this. Knowing what you sell makes marketing a lot easier. Knowing what you *really* sell becomes the cornerstone of marketing in an authentic way. As an entrepreneur, you probably describe your service or product more or less like others in your field—at a surface level. A business coach sells business planning, a bookkeeper sells financial recording, and a music teacher sells music lessons. Why do your clients come to you instead of another company down the street? In reality, your clients are getting something deeper than what you may think you're selling, and you should know that. It becomes the real point of differentiation between you and other businesses providing a similar service or product.

This is about landing on the "what" you do. It's related to your "why" in that often your why, or the reason you want to make a contribution in the first place, drives you to create your what. To best describe your what, or what you really sell, the trick is to drill down to the essence of what you provide for your clients. It's most powerful when it's one word, but two words or a short phrase will work.

For example, on the surface, I sell marketing. Like other marketers, I offer knowledge and experience about how to market—what to say and where to say it to get interest in your business. But, there's something deeper. At this deeper level, I sell growth, which is clearly related to my personal why of nurturing growth. My clients come to me to grow their businesses via their marketing. When you hire me, it doesn't end there. Over the process of our work, my clients also grow their professional selves, and ultimately, their personal selves. The essence of what I sell is growth, and I provide the nurturing support and strategy to achieve it.

When you know the essence of what you sell, you know how to message your marketing. It makes it easier to market what you do because you have a built-in theme for your messaging—your graphics, your language, indeed, your entire brand. When your marketing message expresses your essence, it makes it easier for people to recognize whether you are the right fit for them. The bookkeeper who sells balance becomes an ideal match for some, while the one who sells confidence will draw in others. When you communicate your essence, you know how to approach the world in a way that others can truly understand you and what you sell. The payoff? People are much more responsive to your authentic self than they are to the surface you.

Once you pinpoint what you're selling, step into it. Embrace it. Own it. Lean on it. Use it to guide your marketing for greater results.

If you don't know for sure what you really sell, then find out!

FIND YOUR TRUTH

Talk to your clients, your family, your friends, and colleagues. They see what you offer more easily than you do. Or hire someone to help you. Once you have some insights, try on the words or phrases. Dabble, experiment, and be open until the right description settles on you a little more comfortably than the rest. Knowing and articulating your essence makes all the difference. It's the first step to growing yourself and your business. Get ready for transformation!

Here are several approaches to help you understand what you really sell:

1. Think about one or two of your most successful clients. Ones that you feel really got a lot out of working with you and who you enjoyed working with. If you think about where they started before working with you and where they ended up, how would you describe that journey? Free-write on this topic for a few minutes. Afterwards, go back and circle any words or phrases that seem like possible clues to the essence of what you sell.

2. Think of several clients and the actual outcomes they've had with you. List those outcomes. For example, maybe they finished their taxes, straightened out their books, or launched a new service. Maybe they updated their wardrobe, landed a new client, or refreshed their website. In other words, what did working with you give them on a practical level? Now review each client, and muse on whether there was an emotional piece to the job. Did your client get their taxes done and feel relieved? Or, straighten out their books and feel more organized? Do this for each client and look for a strand of commonality among them.

3. If you are having trouble identifying what you sell, try this idea to get your juices flowing. First, decide which industry you work in. Try to put it into the most generic category. For example, if you are a bookkeeper, then your industry is finance.

If you are a realtor, your industry is real estate. If you are a coach, it depends on what type of coaching you do; a health coach is part of the health industry, a leadership coach might be part of the business industry, and a life coach likely would identify with the personal-improvement industry or family services industry. It doesn't matter so much that you choose the right industry, or want to look at multiple industries, as this is just a creative research exercise to find some inspiration. Once you've chosen an industry, then do some general research on this industry. For example, type "finance industry" in a web search and read a couple of the articles that describe this industry. Visit some of the websites that come up. Do you see words or phrases that you identify or resonate with? By depersonalizing your work and looking at the broad strokes of industries you are connected to, you may more easily see the essence of what you do.

5

CLEAR YOUR PATH FORWARD

You can only be real in your business and marketing when you have a business that fits the real you. But sometimes we find there are bits and pieces in our way. We want to make it fit but how do we do that when the task at hand feels uncomfortable? Or when we don't feel like it? There are many parts of running our businesses that may not be our favorite. This is especially true in marketing. We must tackle all the necessary tasks in our business, even if they don't feel good in the moment. Often I find that what doesn't feel good is not the task itself, but how the small business owner is framing that task. Which would you rather walk down: a path littered with obstacles, blocks, and frustrating dead ends? Or one that is clear, relatively easy, and has fun surprises around each corner? Let's look at some ways of clearing your marketing path so that you can move forward more easily.

Lose the Contradiction

If I say "whistle while you work," what pops into your mind (besides the seven dwarfs)? We immediately understand not only what it means, but why it's desirable. Work and leisure (or pleasure) are related, after all. We generally do one to get the other. Work seems mandatory, i.e., working for the means to get those things that are pleasurable. We now know leisure and pleasure are mandatory for good health and well-being, but they can be out of reach when you don't have enough money to take time off or fund pleasurable activities. Hence, the intertwined relationship.

Being fulfilled in our work makes sense since this gives us pleasure at work and affords us pleasure after work. Too often we pit moneymaking against pleasure time. No one does this more than we girls with big personal lives. We often agonize over the time we spend away from our personal commitments. We create a polarization: work versus fun. Anything that's versus becomes at best, competitive, and at worst, antagonistic. That's a difficult vibration to live in, day after day. Competition creates a winner and a loser. Antagonism has two parts: the antagonist and the agonizer. Who wants either of those as colleagues?

If you've ever been in therapy, acted in theater improv, or seen a martial art like Aikido or Jujutsu that uses a concept of yielding, you've seen a different way to work with competing energies. Have you ever had a seeming contradiction in your world that worked itself out over time, without either side being right and the other wrong? You hold both concepts as equal without directing a lot of attention to them. You make space for both things to possibly be true. Over time, the tension that existed between the two dissipates. What was seemingly unresolvable becomes integrated as true or acceptable.

For example, let's say you dislike updating your website.

CLEAR YOUR PATH FORWARD

You know it needs to be done, but every time you sit down to do it, you feel irritated or distracted. Therefore, you rarely do it, or if you do, there's an afternoon or more of irritation in your world. There are lots of conversations in your head about this whole issue. Why do you do this every time? What's the big deal anyway? Why can't you just do it without all the drama? Or, why do websites have to be updated so often? Why can't business stuff just be easier? Maybe you share all these thoughts with a friend at happy hour, or complain about it to your spouse, or make jokes about how inept you are.

All in all, it takes up a lot of space and does not bring any ease into your work life. Another way to do this would be to admit, with no judgment, you have competing, almost opposite desires, in this situation. On one hand, you'd like to have your website updated and at its best. You have a longing for professional, current business materials that make you look good to others. On the other hand, you cannot stand the process that makes them possible. It gets right under your skin and truth be told, you never want to touch your website again.

Admitting both these positions might seem hopeless or at least a little weird. Taught to be rational, most of us are uncomfortable admitting something as irrational as wanting opposite things. If you are honest about your opposing thoughts and can hold both thoughts with no judgment around having them, there will start to be a resolution. At first it will just be a softening around the whole situation. Neither truth will seem bigger than the other, and you may experience a bit of resignation. At some point, when held long enough, the two will cease to feel like they are in opposition. As crazy as it may seem, you admit that both are really true and that it's OK. You realize you do have to make some choices to either let the website stand unchanged or put in some time to update it. Drama won't fuel your viewpoint any longer. You'll make decisions that you feel more at peace about and likely, the website will get updated either by you or someone you hire to do it.

Truly, magic happens when we make room for both.

Why? It makes room for us to be our whole, messy selves. It's hard to be authentic when you are trying to ignore your constant tension. Studies show that we humans are uncomfortable when we hold contradictory beliefs.[7] Psychologists call it cognitive dissonance.

For example, if you think spending time in your personal life is better than your time at work but spend a lot of time working, you are likely to feel uncomfortable during your workday. If you believe pleasure should be enjoyed only after work completes, you may find it difficult to create personal relaxation and pleasure time in your personal life, since as an entrepreneur, there is always more work you could do. Or if you believe sales people are unsavory, you are likely to experience uncomfortable tension between selling (which you may feel is slimy) and your desire to make your business successful. You may find yourself not only avoiding sales conversations, but also not doing needed marketing activities that might lead to these sales conversations to avoid this tension.

This goes beyond the typical resistance many entrepreneurs have to doing something out of their comfort zone. When faced with cognitive dissonance, we feel so uncomfortable we seek to change beliefs or behaviors to bring ourselves back into congruence. For example, instead of supporting ourselves in growing into a more productive attitude about sales, we may rationalize our not getting to the needed marketing activities with thoughts of being too busy, needing more research, or being unsure what exactly we need to do, which acts to keep us away from the tension. I see many entrepreneurs avoiding some area of their marketing or sales because of these contradictory beliefs when instead they could overcome them if they would step toward their real feelings on the subject.

Combatting the contradictory beliefs not only doesn't work, it makes you inauthentic. Being authentic means looking at all of yourself. The more you deny or ignore the contradiction, the more control it has over your actions. The answer lies in *allowing* the contradiction to come to light and working with it, not against it. Yielding style martial arts work because no energy goes to resisting. By allowing the attack, the receiver need only exert a little energy in moving the attack to her advantage. She doesn't block or return the attack initially, but inserts herself into the attack in a way that uses the energy of the attack itself to knock the attacker off balance. In this way, the need for a counter attack can be minimal or goes away entirely. *Flowing with* creates less resistance and in turn, needs less energy on your part to respond. Therapy and coaching both have many tools to create this state, too.

Use "Yes, and..."

Another approach to working around our resistance to tasks we don't love comes from the "Yes, and …" approach, popular in theater improv trainings. It's common to see improv training used in corporate or leadership settings to help executives become better decision makers. Improv classes have been taught at Duke, Columbia, UCLA, Harvard and MIT Sloan, and used by companies such as American Express, DuPont, Ford, PepsiCo, and Procter & Gamble, Twitter, Google, and Fidelity. People who take improv classes improve their ability to listen, go with the flow, and manage the unexpected. They tap into their creativity and are better at teamwork. Saying "no" stops the action and so does "Yes, but…" With improv training, the negative goes away. You learn the positives of failure and how to cope when something doesn't work. These traits are needed for successful entrepreneurship.

The "Yes, and …" approach simply means that no matter what happens around you, your response must always be "yes, and," at which point you add new ideas and comments. You aren't allowed to say "no" or "yes, but …" This works in comedy improv with hilarious results. It works in your business in more serious ways.

This technique creates acceptance. It shows you how to not push against what is. When you can live life in terms of seeing what's happening and only adding to it, you are both stepping into flow and accepting that while reality may not be what you want it to be, you can only build on the reality of the present. Using this accepting approach can restore harmony to our day-to-day life. It lets us be our whole selves, interacting with others in positive, life-affirming ways.

This doesn't just affect us. We are each involved with circles of people—our families, friends, co-workers, and communities—that are all affected by our participation with them. If everyone runs around with this energy of contradiction, it creates a group, nation, possibly a globe of people who are in resistance to their own lives. The skills used in improv can help you feel safe in a group because you learn that no matter what, you're all working together. "Yes, and…" can increase your ability to make a contribution as you learn to toss in your ideas. You realize trust comes from building upon each other's ideas rather than negating one another and striving to have your ideas be right. This is an approach that honors everyone's authenticity.

Don't aim to just feel better about workday tasks that feel like a pain. Overcoming what we don't love to do and making it easier is often the key ingredient to success. Success at work creates part of the means and *meaning* for our lives. We all long to contribute to ourselves and our community. Your work steps in as a primary way to do that. Winning looks like being happy and grateful for the work you do each day, feeling as though your work fits with and supports the personal life you love, and getting the success you're longing for as the real you.

Your livelihood should support the real you

When enough of us as individuals win, all of humanity begins to win. We are empathic beings who are collective by nature. We are biologically, emotionally, and spiritually primed to take in the attitude or vibration of the people around us. If you're a parent, you see this in action when you realize parenting happens by modeling, not talking. If you are surrounded by people with attitudes of defeat and despair, you have a high chance of feeling similar. Ditto if the people around you are happy and in their bliss because of the contribution they are making. In other words, as we begin to lift people up, it creates a ripple effect, and many people are lifted up.

Speaking of uplifted—happier people are healthier, experience less stress, and live longer. Don't believe me? Google it for yourself. Today I found 14 studies that said just that. Happy people have reduced risk of heart disease, stronger immune systems, less physical pain, and live longer lives than those who are unhappy.[8]

As I sit here writing, I found 101 pages of books when I typed in "happiness" on Amazon. At 12 to 16 books per web page, that's a lot of information on how to be happy! This goes beyond health and wellness. Happier people develop more resiliencies to cope with what's not working, transform their lives for the better, and head towards a flourishing life.[9]

What does this mean for the collective planet? Happy people tend to give more to charity, do more volunteer work, and participate in their community. They are less cautious dealing with others, believing most people are fair and helpful.[10] They are more productive at work, more creative at solving problems, and better at negotiating.[11] People who experience negative emotions, on the other hand, tend to act in opposite ways. They get stuck and live in states of stress, which encourage them to attack or flee.[12] Imagine a world where we profoundly shifted our frequency.

Here's what came in when I was receiving information in the beginning of writing this book:

If you shift the frequency of activities on your planet, you will be able to shift the frequency of the planet. Instead of violence happening frequently, peace can flourish. Instead of depression spreading, happiness can. Instead of abuse, safety. And, on and on. The importance of up leveling your frequency cannot be understated. You have a collective history of focusing on what doesn't work. You must shift this to see what does work, so that you can increase it. By spending your days immersed in practices that lift your heart, feed connection, and bring ease, you will change the collective experience.

It's true that each of us has a personal opportunity as well as the collective one just discussed. This can be something you are called to do to enhance other's lives or the environment around you. It encompasses every possible contribution you can make, big and small. Your job comes in finding yours and, to the best of your ability, moving it forward.

Questions for Reflection:

- Can you name any contradictions you hold related to marketing?
- Is it possible to hold both of these contradicting points

as true for you?
- Can you imagine getting to "yes, and…" about these contradictions?

Discover How Family Ties Can Bind

One of the most effective ways to find your authentic self is to break family patterns. If you look back through the generations of your family, you might see a long line of behaviors such as: money mishandling, dysfunctional communication, illness, anger management issues, depression, passive aggressive or control issues, workaholism, neglect, intimacy issues, playing below one's potential, lack of boundaries, alcohol or drug use, unplanned children, abuse, crime and so on, persisting across the generations. If you can step back far enough with an objective eye, you can name the patterns existing in your family. These are the issues the group you've come to be part of has chosen to explore, work with, and know intimately.

> *Enrique grew up in a family that has a wide range of behaviors around clarity in pursuing one's own path. Because they are from Central America, which has a reputation for being both laid back and overly enmeshed with family influence, it's easy to say it's a cultural thing. However, friends of Enrique's family don't display this same range of patterns around self-determination. Among the siblings of each generation of his family, there seem to be three personality types: the pursuer, who determines what he wants and does it; the actor, who doesn't pursue her own dream but supports other's dreams by her actions; and the victim, who believes their own circumstances are too difficult to accomplish much of anything.*
>
> *They act this pattern out over and over, with every generation.*

It's not even one side of the family—the marriages that take place within the family bring in other families, who also have this pattern. This, of course, impacts their work lives, as some members of the family pursue their work dreams as entrepreneurs, while others are busy working to make other's dreams come to fruition, and still, others aren't working at all. This pattern shows up in their monetary lives also, as some in the family build wealth, others maintain it, and others spend it. The first two times Enrique tried to become an entrepreneur, the pressures of this pattern were too difficult to overcome. He struggled to believe that he could not only decide his own future, but also bring it into being. He eventually went to work for a corporation that allowed him a fair amount of autonomy. He's splitting the supporter role vs. the dream-builder role in this job, as some things are under his direction and some things are supporting others. For now, he chooses this compromise—some structure and stability mixed with some self-determination—while he works to overcome this family pattern. His hope is to let enough of the pattern go so that he can someday step into his own business in a healthy way.

Whatever your family's patterns, every generation makes strides to overcome them. Some make large steps, others tiny. It's the attempt that matters. When you feel as though you are going it alone, remember you are part of a collective, and every member in your group does their part to move it along. Even the ones who are doing something bad are part of the process, as these folks may have agreed to be instigators within the group, so that others could do their growth work. You may not always like it, but you can celebrate that you are part of a bigger whole, where everyone shares the need to grow around a similar issue.

If you keep participating within this whole, it will keep

moving forward. Sometimes it looks like stepping away when it's expected you'll stay, so that another may feel the loss and be moved to reflect on how it happened, rather than sitting back and blaming. Or, if they choose to blame, you get to demonstrate that hurtful behaviors will no longer be tolerated. Other times it may look like changing your own expectations or forgiving others. In other words, if you are continuing to assess, digest, and act on what's happening within the group, you are doing your part.

Why does this matter to your marketing? Family patterns don't just apply to your personal life. The beliefs the generations of your family hold about money, working, independence, trust, communication, and self-worth directly contribute to your ability to be successful in running your own business. I saw this so often in my clients that I became a coach, rather than consultant, so that I had the training and tools to help them through these issues. That's why I tell all my clients that if you're going to grow your business, you have to grow yourself. Why? Because, you aren't the person you need to be to run that larger business. I explain to them: Here you are, the size you are, and the size your business is. Over here is where you want your business to grow. But, you aren't that person yet! So, you have to become that person—the one capable of running, managing, selling, and fulfilling in that new, larger business. Doing that often means growing beyond the limiting, defeating, critical stances you may have inherited from your upbringing.

- How do you know if you have a family pattern to overcome in your marketing? You may experience reactions like these from others:
- **Direct:** Parents or family members who fear you won't make it if you own your business rather than work for a company. Raised in a generation that valued the safety or

financial security companies seemed to promise, this family member worries you're taking the wrong path. This comes up around your marketing, as that's the most visible place in your business. Here are some ways this plays out: family members see your email about your next course or upcoming talk, and call you to see if you're sure about this business. Or, they sigh and look distressed when you speak about your work, tell you about jobs they've heard of, or send contacts to you of people they believe could give you a company job, even in a different industry.

- **Indirect:** Family members may not talk about your business at all, though this smacks of the same fears as the direct approach. They ask how you are, how the kids are, about your health, and tell you all their updates without once ever mentioning your work life. When you bring it up, it's met with vague responses, like "that's good" or "oh, interesting" with no follow-up conversation. You are left feeling like the invisible person in a room full of others.

- **Joking:** Your comments or discussions about your work are met with light teasing or meant-to-be funny comments. This might sound as though the person is interested or supportive, but if you look back on the conversation, there was no substance exchanged. Even when it seems like they are asking in earnest, they ask with a joking comment that, if you listen to the actual words, could be interpreted as critical. Something like, "Hey, how's life for my favorite self-employed slacker?" Or, when you are explaining something about the business, you may hear, "Oh, must be really hard working whenever you want to," or some other joking comment instead of responding to what you are saying. This approach may seem harmless, but also indicates a fair level of discomfort, either in a fear for you or a comparison for them, as they fight back their own desires for more autonomy or living their dream.

Or you may experience this from yourself:

- **Self-sabotage:** When you are thinking about a new service, preparing for a presentation to get new business, or doing some other marketing effort, you have an internal reaction that seems like one of the above. You either directly question your abilities or your reasons for being in business. You may express doubt about the sanity or safety of this effort. You may find yourself asking if it's time to get a real job. Or, you disconnect from yourself and feel numb, unable to access your ideas and creativity, unable to bring yourself to focus on the marketing piece. Or, you push on, making jokes to yourself and others, about what you're up to.
- **Marking time:** You keep taking steps in your marketing but nothing seems to work out. Every time you start to gain momentum, you find yourself pulling back or getting overly stressed. It seems as though you should be making more progress, but somehow you aren't. Or you've been having successes, but at some point, they stop cold, and you are left at the same level of success you've had for a while.
- **Overwork:** You are making progress in your marketing efforts, but they take a lot of work. Each effort brings more business but also more work, and you wonder if you can keep going. You are busy but not taking steps to do things differently, like setting up systems, so that you can be more graceful with your time and efforts. You might consider growing your business, but dismiss it because that would require much more work and that marketing effort. You are not energized by your efforts, but rather, feel drained.

If you identify with something in this list, it's likely you inherited some family beliefs about money, success, or safety that are holding you back. You'll need to address these head on and recover from them to grow. Even the first three, which are enacted by other people toward you, rather than something you are bringing up, mean you have some work to do. A family member will only act in these ways toward you when on a subconscious level you are asking them to.

These steps can help you begin to untie the family cords holding you back:

1. **Identify the way it's showing up from the list above.** Ask yourself what family patterns are playing out to cause this reaction, either from the other person or inside yourself. If you don't resonate with what's listed above, but think you may have family issues at play, start paying attention to what family ties may be impacting in your business today.

2. **Let the outside world answer your question about what family patterns are at play.** Live with the question over the next few days. You may find yourself recalling phrases from your family, life, or situations around money or work that were playing out as you grew up. You might have a dream connected to this question. You might read an article or find a book that brings something to mind. Trust what comes to you if it seems to answer this question.

3. **Take time to journal or discuss this idea with someone you trust.** Often, I muse to my spouse or friend during a questioning time like this, and they see something I don't. Or, while writing in a journal without censoring yourself, you may suddenly start remembering important issues.

4. **When you see what some of the inherited patterns are, decide to deal with them directly.** If the patterns are about money, consider educating yourself about finance so that you have a more realistic view of it, or work with a financial counselor to make plans and budgets for your goals. If the patterns are about success, consider therapies and healing modalities that deal with self-worth. If you have family patterns that are related to safety, then you may need to heal from trauma or abuse that happened earlier in your life, or in

your parent's lives.

Take regular action on healing these patterns. They do not go away if left unattended, and in my experience, wreak havoc on entrepreneurs' business lives. The authentic marketer in you may be buried under here. Why not devote some of your non-working hours to bolstering yourself and show up clean and clear in your business?

Questions for Reflection:

- Can you name any patterns that run through your family line?
- How do these patterns hold you back or cause havoc in your marketing?
- What actions can you take to heal these patterns?

Play for Results and Move Ahead

Our culture's story of success centers on success being hard to obtain. We often think that it's going to take more than we have to get it. Or that it might be for other people but not us. Or that the only way to get it is to be someone we are not.

I want you to know that it doesn't have to be that way. This myth helps us stay comfortably seated where we are, rather than pursuing the changes that, even though they might make us happy, might also feel very uncomfortable while we are making them. Think about every fairy tale or hero's journey you've ever read. Although they enjoy a happy ending, would any of the main characters have agreed to their journey beforehand? No way. It's similar with our journey toward authenticity. Although the end might be worth it, the pathway there will be rife with challenge and change.

In coaching we look at playing for results rather than getting to a goal. In this way, your focus moves away from the uncomfortable feelings that can arise when doing what we don't like to do and toward the future you are trying to create. You bypass any resistance you have to change and start looking at your actions and the results they create. Your focus is on *affecting matter* rather than making change. What does this mean? Let's start by defining matter—you know, the stuff they defined in 8th grade science class as the physical things all around us.

Matter differs from energy. This is a good distinction for purpose-driven folks who tend to focus on energy more than physical matter. Often in our quest to contribute, we tend to focus on the energetic. But as Pierre Teilhard de Chardin said, we are spiritual beings having a physical existence—with emphasis on the physical as the full other half of being spiritual. In this arena that we all call life, it turns out we interact most with energy in the physical plane.

How does this happen in marketing? Exactly the same—you need to focus on playing for results. If the focus centers on what you can create rather than only outcomes, then you have a better chance of moving forward.

Nina was just starting a new marketing campaign when she and I met. Recognizing I might have a piece she was missing, she asked if we could have a phone conversation to discuss where she was in the beginning of her new effort. In a few short minutes, I sensed she was feeling overwhelmed, alone, and completely exhausted by all that needed to be done to have a successful outcome for her campaign. Her problem wasn't that she couldn't see what needed to be done; it was that she was approaching all that needed to be done as an obligation that carried great consequences if things didn't go well. In addition, a lot of what needed to be done was not in her skill-set, or were tasks she really didn't like doing. No wonder she was exhausted!

She hired me during that call, not so much because I had the correct credentials in marketing, but because I pointed out a way for her to get more support in doing the things that weren't her sweet spot. I helped her see that if she fully showed up and played with getting results on many small tasks, she could, indeed, meet the goals of her campaign. She cried with relief during our conversation that someone could see her tired, parched soul struggling to do something important in her business, but going about it in a way that would only bring her the very thing she feared—failure. Instead of taking on the whole project and slugging through it with drudgery, she started looking at what result she could create with the next task. Within five days, she found some friends and colleagues who were willing to brainstorm with her, keep her accountable, remind her to have fun, and to do her activities from love. She creatively found a way to fund an assistant to help her with the administrative parts of the project that previously made Nina want to hide under her bed. Now, she could turn her attention to where she had the most power: making connections with the people who could fund her campaign.

Not that stepping into this part of the campaign was easy for Nina. She had to work through issues around not bothering others, and ideas around needing the support of others. This meant she no longer focused on getting it right, but now could focus on affecting changes in one part of the campaign, instead of being overwhelmed with the whole. She began to experiment or play with affecting the outcome of just the next call or the next few hours, which freed her up to be herself and start enjoying the moments. The results speak for themselves: not only was her campaign a success (she earned more than she had planned), but she also had a newfound confidence in connecting with others, and was offered a record deal for the album she was funding.

Do these results sound amazing? You bet. In truth, all of us have the potential of meeting or exceeding our goals, but most of us stop ourselves when feeling overwhelmed and not getting the support we need. Rather than break our focus down to the next small action we can take, or look at our business and efforts with playfulness and ease, we focus on all that's not going well.

But no small business or small business owner can survive the amount of negativity that comes when they focus on what's not working or what could go wrong. Instead, a more positive approach is needed.

In coaching, this tool is called *playing for results* and it looks at breaking down a project into goals and outcomes and experimenting to see how you might meet those goals. Your focus shifts to not whether you meet those goals, but how the actions you're taking are bringing results that either propel you toward the goal or push you away from it. If you can bring in the discipline of not getting caught in the story of what it will mean to meet or not meet your goal, you can be more present in the actions you're taking. Being neutral about whether the actions are moving you toward or away from the goal gives you more power to take different actions and change directions more easily. You aren't as concerned with where you end up as you are with the journey that takes you there. This path lets you stay in your authentic nature of a creator rather than a victim of circumstance.

Here's an exercise on playing with matter in marketing to get results and move forward powerfully:

1. Pick one small marketing goal in your business — one you're not sure how to reach.

2. Brainstorm—by yourself or with your coach or a colleague—many ideas that might move you toward that

goal. Go for ten ideas at least! Twenty would be even better. Choose several of these ideas and experiment with enacting each idea over the coming week.

3. Treat it like a game you are playing. Track whether the actions you take on each idea move you toward your goal or not. Remember, don't judge whether the movement is good or not! You want to keep as neutral a response as you can.

- If the actions are not moving you toward your goal, how can they be changed to get a different result?
- If they are moving you toward your goal, do you need to keep doing them or could it be time for another action to come in?
- If you can't answer these questions, have a colleague or coach listen to you talk them out. Chances are you do have the answers, you just might not be hearing them from yourself.

4. This continual focus on taking actions in your business to see if they move you forward or backward instead of whether they get the end result, can be a great discipline for a successful business. It can strip away some of the anxiety, and free up space for more enjoyment and creativity. Try it and see for yourself. If you'd like, download a worksheet at lindabasso.com/theauthenticmarketer.

This concept can be used to move us along in our overall business as well. We often shy away from addressing something that seems uncomfortable or difficult to change. Rather than make a plan that includes experimenting with different approaches that gets us a new outcome, we throw our hands up and say it's just this way. This can keep us stuck in routines that don't work with our rhythms, processes, and activities that drain our energy, and a feeling of futility in our businesses rather than excitement. Successful businesses find a way to move forward through difficult situations.

We are very powerful when we play with matter. Trouble is, we don't often spend time deliberately affecting things, because we spend too much time worrying about what's the matter. A little humor with my words, but don't overlook my point. You are here to enact a difference with matter. Yet, so many of us are afraid to act or don't use the info coming back to us to change how we engage with matter.

For example, take a person or situation you are having difficulty with in your business. Instead of playing with the situation as if you were a creator and could affect an outcome and create different results, you push the situation away. You tell yourself you don't have time or that you shouldn't have to deal with this person or situation. We are still in a plane where every action has an opposite reaction; as you push this situation away, they come forward more strongly. You may find that it takes up much of your attention and thinking. If, instead, you bend toward the situation, they will begin to bend away from you freeing up your energy. This matters to the entrepreneur because often we have difficulty with our vendors, assistants, or other support people. Or we are distracted at work by a personal interaction that is difficult.

Just how do you bend toward a person or situation that you are upset by? Start by first accepting that you want to deal with the situation, not run from it. Just giving yourself the permission to step toward it brings in your power. Then, use the tools you have available to you, like changing your interior state with journaling or meditation, prayer, intention, or energetic clearing. Don't only keep engaging with it on a superficial, physical level where you make it about right and wrong. As you clear out your personal feelings and what gets stirred up by the person or situation, you will find it starts to untangle and bother you less. Use all your senses to engage in matter and the situation, and

CLEAR YOUR PATH FORWARD

be impressed with your ability to create different results. As we did in the exercise above, you can brainstorm different actions that could move you toward a different outcome. As you begin to play for different results, you will begin to experience different outcomes. This forward movement is much more powerful than being stuck in the upset.

Bringing this all back to your marketing, begin playing with matter to see what results you get instead of only outcomes. Matter can be other people. Make a connection and see where it goes. Your collateral counts as matter. Make some and see what response you get. The web makes a perfect place for it; make something online, and push it out to see where it goes and what comes back. This approach keeps the underpinnings of your efforts loose and energetic—and away from perfectionism.

If you can step into playing with these bits of matter with actions and results to see what occurs, you can create a sense of flow, and all those pesky to-dos on your marketing list can feel easier and more organic, rather than a long, never ending list. You can't have your marketing wrapped up in what you are worth, or being accepted or rejected. That's not what it's about. It's about playing with matter for results and seeing what happens as you move powerfully forward.

Questions for Reflection:

- Do you tend to focus on the results instead of the process?
- If you focused on creating results instead of arriving at outcomes, could that lighten your marketing journey?
- Are you willing to take direct action toward a situation you want to shift in your business?

Realize You're in the Right Place

I see the marketplace changing. Rather than buying from faceless companies, many of us will choose to work with and purchase only from those we find appealing in some way, or somehow, believe in and trust to solve our issues. Rather than just buying something, we want to come together with others whose products or services can add to what we're doing. I believe that we'll no longer make our decisions based solely on practical senses but rather a feeling of resonance.

As a business owner, it's important that you, too, show up in a way your clients can resonate with. For successful marketing, you need to be your best brand ambassador, and to do this you must believe that you're in the right place at the right time. It won't work if you are sitting in regret for not being here faster or that you aren't as far as you should be.

There's Nothing the Matter with You

I often hear clients asking, "What's the matter with me?" when something doesn't go the way they thought it would, or they see others having success and they are not. Please know this: there may be new behaviors or actions or there might be different outcomes you need to create, but there is never anything intrinsically wrong with you. This question comes as an unfortunate side effect of living in a culture that doesn't affirm our authentic goodness. There are a few reasons for this:

1. Our culture tends to focus on the things we achieve outside of ourselves like where we end up, rather than enjoying the process of getting there. There are few stories about the path it takes to get somewhere and a lot of focus on the success stories of those who made it. Instead of growing up learning about how to use your authentic nature to move forward, you

probably grew up wondering how to finally arrive where you wanted to go and possibly feeling uncomfortable about where you were in the process.

2. All of us reach a time in our adolescence when we realize we are alienated from the people around us. This is a natural, biological part of becoming an independent adult. Traditional cultures handled this natural occurrence with rites of passage to help teens find their authentic selves through this transition, but our modern life has stripped this away. If teens don't come through this period with a reconnection to their sense of who they really are on a profound level, evidence shows this creates a deep emptiness that drives them to fill the void with substances and behaviors that don't really get at the itch. They're left with the feeling that something feels amiss.

3. A third reason involves the way many of us had some kind of dysfunction happening as we grew up. Maybe there was substance abuse—ranging from social drinking to alcoholism—or emotionally distant family members, or those who were unskilled in communication. Perhaps your parents were highly judgmental, overly righteous, or too strict. Possibly, you saw the adults around you model being passive victims instead of powerful people. Or, you simply had caregivers that focused on your physical existence without a thought to your emotional or spiritual sides. Whatever your flavor of childhood angst, life didn't feel right. As a result, that question—What am I doing wrong?—kept surfacing. You concluded that you must have something wrong with you, you're not good enough, not lovable, not wanted, and on and on. Instead of learning that your authentic self was lovable as is, you may have blamed it for the responses you got from your environment.

As you can see, each of these is about our circumstances and not about us. Yet, as we discussed earlier, the need to belong puts us in a difficult situation. We are likely to let the group we belong to shape our point of view about ourselves rather than reach inward and rest on our authentic nature. To find your authenticity within your business, you must do the inner growth work needed to separate who you really are from the thinking you were handed by your culture, community, or family.

Additionally, something curious happens when you focus on playing for results. It's almost never a straight line between you and what outcome you are trying to affect. Things often meander when you are moving toward what you want. You see a goal, start playing for results to achieve it, and then, either life intervenes or you get distracted or become fearful. Things go to the left, then right, and later, you may find yourself back on or near your original path, wondering what in the heck happened!

This can certainly cause us to question if we have something wrong with us, or at least our approach.

Why does this happen in this way? Because although you think in a linear fashion, the universe does not move in one. Instead, it moves in more of a circular, spiral effect and, to be honest, with plenty of chaos. This can be terrifying to you now, but as you increase your consciousness, you'll find it not so difficult to thrive within. This all begins to make total and complete sense—just not in the way you currently see time and space.

There are many realities and sets of time happening at the same time. As a result, it often takes more than a straight line to connect two or more things. Some weaving of experience and people sometimes have to happen first in order to bring about the correct or highest outcome.

Similarly, this concept can also make some things happen instantaneously: You think you'd like to do something, and voila, the very person or thing you need arrives on your doorstep. That's because when things are aligned, energy can be moved from one set of time through the layers into another by reaching through.

Here are some principles that can help us navigate the circuitous nature of the cosmos.

1. **You can never be in the wrong place.** Many of you are in jobs or life experiences you want to change, yet you don't want to change your state of mind or integrate the situation in a way that satisfies the learning you originally wanted from the situation. As a result, you stay or repeat the experience until you do. If you grasp that you are never, ever in the wrong place, you can stop obsessing about why you got there, or why you can't leave and get to the business at hand. Make the best of the situation for now so that you can learn what you need from the situation.

2. This may create resistance in many of you, but there's only one other choice: continue to rail against the present and be unhappy. Instead, **make the best of the situation and at least experience some measure of peace.** By shifting your attention toward how to make things even slightly better, you are starting from what is. This puts you in the only power position in the universe. Tremendous capacity exists in the present moment, which explains why presence and mindfulness are being talked about so much these days.

3. **In this powerful spot, you begin creating something new.** It may feel only slightly new, which can feel disappointing, but I promise if you begin to master this at the level where you are right now, you will move forward. Someday, you won't have to make these slight adjustments—but for now, remember you are an apprentice. Start shifting things including external situations, internal beliefs, and thoughts, until the situation becomes easier to tolerate. This creates the only way out:

through the situation. As mentioned above, you are never in the wrong place because a) you can head in any other direction as soon as you'd like and b) the training you are receiving by being in a difficult situation and learning to shift it puts you on the path of becoming a powerful creator.

4. Once you are a powerful creator, you are almost never in situations you consider wrong because **you simply shift things as needed.** This doesn't mean bad things don't happen, or you're never faced with situations requiring courage, or you don't feel sorrow. Powerful creators often deal with all those things in the same day! They are proficient at processing big emotions and enjoy the surfing of life because they have the skill and courage to do so.

5. **Sometimes the things you dream about or want to happen take some weaving.** Since you are asking from one vantage point, you often can't see what's in the way of it coming to fruition. This requires trust. That doesn't mean you can't work toward your dream, but things will never fall into place from your efforts alone. You can only surf waves you are close to. Trust that the weaving will happen toward creating the highest and best outcome. The reason weaving and joining sometimes takes time can come from many of your dreams involving other people or situations that have not yet come to be. This means there are a complicated number of variables that must shift in order to bring the situation into being.

The best way we can deal with this circuitous nature of the cosmos is to affect what you can, and trust in what you can't. This can move you from feeling like a victim of what happens to being in the driver's seat with the universe in your passenger seat as your co-pilot.

Questions for Reflection:

- Do you often wonder if you're where you're "supposed"

- to be in your business journey?
- Can you see there is some weaving taking place in the universe around your business?
- Are you willing to step into the role of a powerful creator and shift your circumstances when needed?

Uncover Your Voice and Style

In the next book of this series, *Love*, we'll look at developing your authentic voice and style as a means of showing your love for yourself and your clients. Here, we'll look at the beginning steps in this journey and just why it's so important.

One of the main ways you can own your worth is in your willingness to share your real voice. Think about it. When you are not sure that you, and by extension your business, are worthy, you aren't going to shout from the rooftop about how great you are. But really, this is exactly what you must do to market your business. This is one of the reasons that growing your business forces you to grow yourself. You must overcome any limiting beliefs you have about yourself and your business's abilities in order to effectively share your true brilliance and get clients.

This journey asks you to find your own voice and style as these convey the real you and how your business is unique. It's the part that makes your messaging authentic instead of salesy and pushy. Sharing in your real voice is how a potential client can see if you are the right fit. Finding your voice and style is kind of where all your marketing comes together. So far you've looked at your truth, your why, and what you really sell. The voice and style you share it with is the part where you language all that inner knowing outward so that others can see it, too.

Where's Your Real Expression Hiding?

We've all grown up with a lot of do's and don'ts around

what we say and how and when we say it. Uncovering all the reasons you thought it wasn't OK to be your full expressive self is a journey with some twists and turns. If your voice or unique style aren't flowing easily, it's usually because you either lack the inner permission or have an unconscious block that isn't letting you see what's in your way. You may be carrying a lot of shoulds about self-expression, be overwhelmed with imposter doubts, or simply are not in touch with your inner voice. Whatever the reason, there is a way out.

You may wonder if the way you are sharing now is your authentic voice and style. Or maybe you are pretty sure that you're being your real self, but wonder if there's another level of you under the surface. Or you may be very sure that the way you write and share about your business is definitely not you.

Wherever you are, trust me that you can find your real voice and style if you are patient and kind with yourself. If your voice or style has gone into hiding, there is certainly a reason why. Uncovering that and coming back to expressing yourself may take some effort and understanding.

I use the word uncover because every single one of us has a unique voice and style. No, you are not going to be the one person on the planet that doesn't end up having one. Each of us has all the resource and expression we need right inside of us, patiently waiting to be let out. It's simply a matter of clearing out what may be in the way.

Here are some common reasons we hide our real voice and style:
- Being criticized or teased about the way we expressed ourselves when younger such as having a learning difficulty such as dyslexia or a speech issue like stuttering.
- Being highly intelligent and getting criticized or teased about it

CLEAR YOUR PATH FORWARD

- Having parents or people around us who aren't comfortable with their own expression
- Being an extrovert growing up surrounded by introverts
- Being an introvert and not knowing it and/or being surrounded by extroverts
- Living in an area where we disagree with the politics, culture, or community values
- Having close relationships with people who don't encourage you to express yourself

If you recognize one of these as impacting you, great! Now you can begin to address it consciously. Just because your environment didn't make it comfortable as a child to express yourself doesn't mean that you can't create the correct circumstances to do it now. Or if you've unconsciously created an environment today that doesn't let you express yourself, it's not too late to make a change. Knowing why you are hiding is the first step toward coming out.

One of the main indicators that you have not found your voice or style is when you envy others who you think have found theirs. You may read someone else's website and think that if only you could express yourself like he or she does, that would be so much better. When you have your voice and style intact, you see others who have theirs in place and feel appreciation and respect, not envy or that you are less than. If you find yourself turning green when noticing someone else's voice and style, that's a clue that yours has been staying out of sight.

Another way you can tell if yours is hiding is by whether you are sharing or not. When working on creating copy or messages, for your website or a blog for example, it's totally normal to feel really bad while you are creating it. Most people feel a range of feelings when writing that go from uncomfortable to downright critical. Even those of us who are writing books or have written hundreds of articles feel this regularly! It's no biggie if you feel like you have nothing to say, or tell yourself while you're writing that what you're writing is terrible and will never take you anywhere. As long as you are also continuing to write through that voice, you're in the normal zone. If you feel that way while you're writing and come back to read what you wrote a little later and think "Hey, maybe that's not as bad as I thought," then you are doing just fine.

Writing or expressing yourself might not feel comfortable which is normal. That doesn't mean you can't do it

---

But if you are letting that critical voice stop you from even writing, or you are writing and never coming back to edit and finish it up, then you are hiding. Or if you know you need to create more in writing but aren't, you are hiding. If you long to give talks in public but never do, you are hiding. If you want to create videos or do online live recordings and aren't, you are hiding. In other words, if you aren't sharing yourself in writing and speaking with others in some way, or in big enough ways, then you are hiding.

If your style is in hiding, rather than your voice, then you likely feel uncomfortable with how you look, dress or style yourself, or with how your marketing materials look. You'll know this is present when you stand in your closet feeling like you have nothing to wear even though you are surrounded by clothing. Or you may find yourself comparing your style to the style of others and feel lacking. Or you are constantly apologizing for the way your marketing materials look. Our style goes into hiding for many of the same reasons as our voice does. Additionally, you may have experienced:

- Being criticized for how you dressed or styled your

hair
- Having a physical feature that was teased or commented on
- Being from a culture that had strict rules about "looks" and dress codes
- Getting criticized for stepping away from the norms in appearance

Whatever the reason, your style can be coaxed out of hiding.

The goal is to feel comfortable enough with your unique style and voice that you are willing to share regularly with others. That creating content, or verbally sharing, feels good enough that you do it as much as your business needs you to in order to have the amount of business that you need. You can walk into your closet and feel great about choosing your outfits for business settings. And you are proud of the marketing materials you've created and feel they reflect the real you. If this isn't you, read on to take first steps in uncovering your voice and style. If you feel comfortable enough, but wonder if there's more of you to find, read on and claim another level of your authentic nature.

Criticism Is the Enemy

We shouldn't have to name this specifically, but oddly enough, we do. You'd think it would be common sense that anything we try to do would be downright difficult or even impossible when it's bogged down with critical, demanding, or unkind comments. But when it comes to expressing ourselves, that's what most of us do. This inexplicable inner voice makes itself known the minute you sit down to write that article, consider that social media live share, or choose what to wear to an important meeting. It says things like, "Who are you to write about this? You don't even have success in this, or have never even..." or fill in the blank with whatever you think makes you hugely unqualified to share what you are about to share. Or, if it doesn't disparage you, it goes on and on about how your reader will never read it, or won't get anything from it, or won't understand it, or any number of truly discouraging thoughts. Or it attacks your style by saying you don't have the looks needed, the right clothing, or good enough marketing materials to put yourself forward.

No wonder we have trouble expressing our real selves!

If you fight the criticism directly, it grows stronger and more determined to show you it knows your weak spots. And since it's internally generated, it does! To battle it directly is exhausting. It uses up all the energy you need to actually create. Imagine a flowing stream pushing up against a blockage of some sort. The pressure of this is most intense at the blockage. It causes all sorts of backups and overflows behind the blockage. It's highly uncomfortable for what's above the block to manage the overflow while the areas below the block aren't getting the water they need. Instead, imagine the water finding a way around the block. Even a little trickle around the sides or over the blockage would eventually wear it away. The pressure is reduced by little bits at first, but as more water is able to come through, bigger chunks of the block are moved away.

We can do the same with criticism. Although I don't believe this nasty voice can ever be fully stopped, it can be greatly reduced by taking action and moving ahead with your expression even though the critical voice is there. In other words, it's not about waiting for the voice to not be there in order to share. Instead, you have to admit that the voice is there, maybe even that it's correct, and decide you are going forward with your expression anyway. The first several times you do this feel just awful. You are conflicted and the words struggle to come out or you feel plain awkward sharing your message with others. But over time, if you are willing to press ahead, the critical voice will realize that it doesn't control your actions. Resigned, it seems to come up less strongly. It still takes a snarky potshot here and there, but overall, it's less of a presence.

We cannot fully stop our inner critical voice, but we can lessen its hold by taking action anyway

---

If you are willing to continue to express yourself despite the criticism, you will find another wonderful thing happening. You realize that you do have something to say. People will let you know that they did get value from what you said or wrote. You will get complimented on your marketing materials. You may even start to look forward to your bouts of expression! The fulfillment that comes from successfully expressing yourself and the business it can bring to you is very worth overcoming this paralyzing habit.

- **Encourage it to come out:** Along with decreasing the criticism by continuing to express yourself anyway, another necessary component is to offer your expression a little bit of loving coaxing to come forward. I used to bribe myself when I first started working on speeches and writing more. If I was willing to sit down and work for a session or get a chunk of it done, then I would get to do something I wanted to do. A walk, a bite of chocolate, or a bath were enticing treats that led me forward. I also made sure that the environment I was writing in was lovely and easy to be in. If it seemed easier or more fun to write in a café, I was there. If the kitchen table called to me over my office, cool. If I felt like long hand writing it in a notebook, ditto. In other words, I treated myself well because what I was doing was hard. When I first started trying to express myself, I felt terrible inside myself, and so I did a lot to try to feel better outside myself with the caveat that I would try to make myself feel better as long as I kept showing up to write. I did not get to feel better by avoiding writing

- **You'll also want to praise yourself for putting in the effort rather than for what you created.** I often felt that what I wrote was probably terrible, but I was grateful and proud of myself for having done it. When you don't make it about the outcome but rather about the process, it's an easier journey. We all get that the journey is more important than the destination, but it's harder to put into practice. Often when we are working on that article or video script, we are thinking about all the outcomes it needs to generate which is a lot of pressure. When focused on the number of clients we need to generate or the email list we are trying to build, our expression can feel full of angst. If instead we can just focus on the act of creating and be curious about what's coming out, we can actually enjoy the act of creating. And happily enough, that's actually when we get better outcomes.

- **Let professionals help you:** At some point I hired a stylist to help me with my clothing, hair, and makeup. I didn't go the traditional route where I was color typed by season but found a stylist who typed by elemental essence. Finding out I was a fire type gave me not only the colors/textures to wear that showed the world the real inner me, it also gave me permission to be the active, fiery, abrupt self that I really am. At some level, that's what owning our real voice and style is all about: having permission to be ourselves. Since a little encouragement can go a long way toward bringing out your voice and style, find ways you can offer it to yourself, or find others who can offer it to you.

- **A grand experiment in seeing:** There's no magic formula for finding your voice and style. In my next book,

Love, I'll offer the next steps for coaxing it out and developing it so that it works for you and your clients. But if you never get started here, you won't be ready for that step. For now, just begin to experiment with finding your voice and style and noting when it's hard to find it. Awareness is the first step in any journey like this. Start noticing both when it flows—like when you are talking with your bestie or on an issue you are passionate about—and when it doesn't. If you can get clear on when it's happening you know where to start working on it. When you know where it's happening, try to identify why from the reasons I stated earlier. Was one of these issues present for you earlier in your life? If so, begin to journal how that was for you, or to contemplate it for yourself. Can you imagine this beginning to shift for you? How would you want it to be instead? It's often not until we admit that something is happening and begin to consider alternatives that it can begin to shift.

You'll know it has come out of hiding when the way you write and share is the same as how you talk and act when you are with close friends or others that you feel comfortable and accepted by. People who've just met you will tell you that they have the same experience with you when you are in person or they are reading your materials or meeting you for the first time. Others may say things like "I was reading that and could totally imagine you saying it" or "Oh, that was so you!" after you've given a presentation or class. So this journey is well worth starting.

Questions for Reflection:

- Are you authentic in your expression and have access to your real voice and style?
- If not, what reasons might yours be in hiding?
- Do you see a path to deal with your inner critical voice?

6
AN AUTHENTIC MARKETING PLAN

Let's cut the mystique around your marketing plan. Basically, it contains what you plan to do in your marketing efforts, where you'll conduct these activities, whom you'll do them with, and when you will do it all. It's that simple.

You may wonder if it can be that easy. The answer is yes. You can find your own way to create a plan that works for you. If you want to do your planning only once a year, go for it. Want to do it more often or only as needed? I'm all for that. Want a formal written one? Great. Plan to keep it on the back of a notebook cover? Fine.

It's not important how you do it but rather that you do it. And not only for the sake of saying you did it. You are looking for enough of a plan so that you feel secure your actions are getting you somewhere. You want to know you've considered

AN AUTHENTIC MARKETING PLAN

your business goals, who you are as a person, and what your resources are to create a good plan for yourself. In the end, you want a plan to guide your actions monthly, weekly, and daily. This is the antidote to shiny object syndrome. When you see business owners who are accomplishing a lot in their business, it's because they have a few goals they are pursuing and the plans in place to do so. If instead, you have vague goals and no plan, you risk following every single new thing that pops up in your world.

> Having a solid plan moves you ahead in a grounded, genuine way instead of frantically going this way and that

We all know how to plan. We do it every day. We plan for the next day by deciding on clothing, meetings, lunch, and maybe even what we'll do after work. We plan for holidays and birthdays—where we'll be, who's bringing what, and about what time. We plan with our vendors and clients to move their projects along. Sometimes, we even plan not to have any plans! In short, in today's society, we are all pretty much plan-making machines.

Then why, when it comes to creating a marketing plan, do small business owners look at their shoes and squirm? Why is there so much confusion around this kind of plan making?

Stop the Confusion

Marketing plans are confusing for two main reasons:

1. There are so many ways to reach clients via marketing that it's difficult to choose. Add to that the pressure most entrepreneurs put on their marketing plan, i.e., it must be brilliant and successful. Since marketing outcomes are not something you can know ahead of time, this pressure is counterproductive. It's like planning for a vacation while

telling yourself that this better be the best trip you've ever taken. Since you can't possibly control that, you're better off approaching your vacation plan guided by your preferences, your resources, your intelligence, and your hopes. Same thing goes for your marketing plan.

2. Entrepreneurs don't like marketing plans because they prefer to let things unroll organically, don't want to seem pushy, and don't want to spell it out in case it doesn't work. These behaviors are fueled by limiting beliefs such as "Only sleazy sales people call potential clients" or "I don't have that skill-set" or "What if it doesn't work?" Not doing a plan can simply be an avoidance mechanism. Their thinking goes something like this: "It's not really avoidance if I haven't spelled it out on paper, right?" I've been told hundreds of times by small business owners that they just want to "let things flow."

> *Darla is an entrepreneur who offers consulting to her clients. In the first three years of her business, she did a lot of networking, public speaking, and sought out referral sources in order to gain clients. Don't get lost in the jargon here. I'm just saying that Darla spent a lot of her time meeting a lot of different people and developing relationships with them. She shared her expertise with them by giving talks at their meetings or in meeting them one-on-one. She did this organically, letting one person lead to another. This led to having enough clients for her small business to get started and pay for a simple lifestyle. She was thrilled the business was working. She loved learning the new skills of connecting people to each other, and enjoyed that she was becoming known in her area. It fit perfectly with her personality of helping others. She even started to like having a little recognition. Darla began to be confident in her skill-set with her clients. They were making progress in their businesses, and Darla got that she was part of that.*

After the first three years, Darla began to feel restless and wanted to make more money. She set her sights on growing her business and serving more clients. However, as she researched different ways other consultants made more money in her industry, she was confronted with paths outside of her experience or skill-set. Those who made more money either had longer and higher priced engagements with their clients, worked with groups of clients rather than individually, or had additional revenue streams beyond consulting, such as books, products, and online courses.

She sought support around having longer/higher priced engagements with her clients, but was confronted with the fact that these engagements required different sales conversations than the ones she was used to. She needed to learn sales skills, and how to present the value of her higher priced packages. She would also need to consciously pursue clients, rather than just letting them seek her out. Instead of sitting down to create a plan and chart the steps needed— including learning new skills and doing more research— Darla chose to keep moving ahead in an organic way, taking a whatever-comes approach. As a result, the additional revenue she hoped for has not manifested.

This is often the case for entrepreneurs committed to letting it flow. Instead, I hope you will be brave and face the parts of your plan you need to grow into. After all, that growth can lead you toward accomplishing the hopes you have for your business and your life. Isn't that worth it?

Make Your Plan

The thing I love about making plans is that it lets you include all the parts of your life that you want to. If you have no plan, you are constantly in reaction mode instead of proactively moving forward. How authentic can you be when you are being reactive and only have the choices being presented to you? When you plan ahead, you can set things up to accommodate your personal preferences, quirks, and design. You have the most influence to shape a situation before it happens able to explore options for doing it this way or that, and plan to take steps that are likely to move it that way. If you wait until the situation is unfolding, it's already going down a particular path and there's less you can do to shape it. Instead, you end up trying to fit into it instead of setting it up to fit around you.

You actually waste considerable energy when you continually avoid creating a marketing plan. Instead, why not use that energy to actually make one? If you can drop into the reframe that planning will actually support building a business that fits the real you, it could feel more worthwhile to create. The following pages include several categories of information you need to gather to create your plan. Even if you're not convinced that you'll do one, read through these and see how much more you'll know about yourself if you do.

Admit Your Financial Goals

Admitting your true financial goals can be hard for purpose-driven entrepreneurs who want to focus more on what they give than get. But giving more than what you have isn't sustainable. Undercharging or over-giving can cause resentment in the long run and won't allow you to give your best service. This causes many service-oriented businesses to flounder. Learn to receive gracefully and remember: The more you are given, the more you can give.

Sometimes it happens in the opposite way. A whole class of would-be entrepreneurs dream of making a ton of money with very little effort on their part. It's not that they don't want to help others or make an amazing contribution, they just also long for a life filled with financial ease and time for the things that make life matter to them. Our culture's emphasis on money as the means to enjoy life fuels this type of daydreaming. Add to that the attention the media pays to instant millionaires: Ideas that go viral! High profile startups/buyouts! The internet is flooded with folks telling you they have the secret to six- and seven-figure business solutions for coaches, healers, and anyone who wants to sell their products/services online. The amount of hype and exaggeration boggles the mind. We used to call them get-rich-quick schemes and warned people to avoid anyone who spoke in those terms. Now people flock to them and then wonder why they feel cheated when the promised goal doesn't pan out.

Even those of us who are trained in business fall prey to this wildly swinging pendulum of financial hopes. It's hard to find realistic advice out there about starting a business, to know how much you need to spend, and when to expect realistic returns. When we do see information that's realistic, it seems so hopeless that we could ever make it. Instead, we may dismiss our dreams or secretly hope we'll be the exception.

Unrealistic ideas also come from what we hear about manifesting. Just visualize what you want! Of course, you can't have what you can't imagine, but you need more than vague notions of financial success. You must get very specific when it comes to money, both in naming what you need and planning for how to get it at various stages of your business. Success comes when your visions are given life with your actions.

Visions without actions are just dreams

I've seen many entrepreneurs suffer under the pressure to

perform at a financial level they are not yet capable of. Instead of guiding their businesses to unfold in a natural, sweet way, they push themselves to make a lot of money—fast. This can undermine their confidence when their business doesn't produce as quickly as they want or need. They may begin to question their skill-set or even if they should be in business at all. Have you ever felt like that? You may simply need more time, patience, and/or outreach. Rushing never gets you anywhere except exhausted. And many business owners give up just before they would have found success. Patience and perseverance are two qualities that all successful people have.

What do you do to get an accurate understanding of your business financial goals?

- **Get accurate advice:** Talk to coaches, consultants, and financial advisors who you trust and see having the lifestyle and business results that you desire. Avoid getting advice from those who have the financial success you want, but not the values or lifestyle that you desire. Avoid advice that seems scammy or overpromises. If it seems too good to be true, it probably is. Your aim is to get realistic advice from a few different sources until you have an accurate understanding of typical returns in your industry and style of business.

- **Get yourself supported:** For many, the above realistic advice seems like "too much" or "too long" for your goals and you'll want to pretend it won't be the same for you. This is the single biggest reason that 50% of small businesses fail. If you can't get your head around the years it takes to build a profitable business, it might not be the path for you. Look at why this is unacceptable to you and solve it. Be willing to create a realistic plan for supporting yourself while your business grows to a sustainable level. You may need a side job, savings, or some other kind of investment in the beginning. Rather than resenting this, you have to be grateful for the structures you have that let you plant and nurture the seeds of your business.

- **Do any needed growth work:** There are two types of growth I often see needed. One is for the person who doesn't love money enough. If money feels uncomfortable to you, or too detailed, or is not the reason you love your business you'll need to do some healing work around this. Why wouldn't you love money as the means to support you and others? There are usually many limiting beliefs to be released here. Another is for the person who loves money too much and uses it to prove their worth or feel safe in the world. That's not a healthy view of money either. It often blocks this business owner from having the needed "beginner's mind" that will let them build the foundation of their business correctly. It puts a lot of pressure on the owner and often paralyzes them or pushes away prospective clients.

Questions for Reflection

- How can you shift your focus from the fast and furious to the small, incremental, and joyful path that's needed to get a business up and running?
- How much time do you need in your schedule for planning and implementing these plans, in addition to serving clients?
- How can you be realistic about what you need to support yourself financially along the way?

Study the Market

Many of my purpose-driven entrepreneur clients cringe when I tell them to take a look at their competition, but please, read this through before you jump to judgment. You need to know the market or industry for your product or service. You have to show how your service or product is different, timely, and desirable in order to get clients. Becoming intimately aware of the set of circumstances that your business exists in is key to an effective plan. Studying your competition can save you time and money, but only if you figure out 1) how you are the same as them 2) how you are different and 3) how to express this so that others can understand.

This is not a rhetorical exercise. Potential customers will ask you all the time how your service or product compares to another service or product that seems similar in their minds. That's the operative phrase: in their minds. Often small business owners are so immersed in their own business that they take this distinction for granted. But your potential customers are not immersed in your point of view. They are barraged with an amazing amount of information, and often must work very hard to understand the best buying choice. That's why it's a great service for you to do the work of knowing how you compare to what's out there and explain those differences honestly. You are helping buyers make a truly good choice for themselves.

> **Share the meaningful differences between you and your competition to be of service to potential clients**

As a culture, we don't hesitate to assess someone's outfit or talk about the people in our neighborhoods, companies, and families. There are even television shows based on this premise of looking at others' lives and comparing them to our own. How funny that in a society so set on comparisons that small business owners hesitate to look at their competition to make decisions because it seems unsavory. Small businesses are actually well served when they share information and grow from it. It moves the whole industry forward.

AN AUTHENTIC MARKETING PLAN

How can you know more about the market containing your service or product? Remember those research papers you had to write in school? Apply the same concept. Research and read. Good news—unless you're writing a formal business plan, you are researching only for your own understanding, not to write a paper with citations.

Have fun with this! If you can hold an attitude of excitement and joy around finding out how fascinating your industry might be, you'll get uplifted by immersing yourself in it. Even those who approach this with dread later tell me they became excited and proud to be part of their industry. It also helps you figure out how you are the same and different from others in your industry. Often when my clients are studying their industry or looking at their competition, they have aha moments about themselves and their business. There's nothing like reading something about someone else and hearing your own agreement—or disagreement—with their position to create clarity for yourself.

How do you know what industry you are in? Sometimes it's obvious. A lawyer is part of the legal industry, an accountant is within the financial industry, and a restaurant owner is part of the hospitality industry. Other times, you need to make some decisions about what you identify with. One health coach might identify more with the coaching industry, while another might lean toward the health/wellness industry, and still another might choose to identify equally with both. Same thing goes for any consultant. If you are unsure, do a little online research to see what you can find and ask other professionals until you find yours. Then read and research until you feel comfortable with your general knowledge of your industry.

Once you know the overall landscape of your industry, you need to look at others who offer to meet the same needs as you do. These are your competitors, but I mean that in the nicest sense of the word. I don't mean they are your rivals. Often my clients resist this step because they don't like the idea that they are in a competitive situation, which usually connotes fiercely vying against one another, winners/losers, or trying to one-up each other. Feel free to use whatever word you like instead. Although competitor literally just means another person or company who's offering a product or service like yours, you may prefer to label them colleagues or another word that doesn't have bad connotations.

If you take the time to study who's around you, what they are doing well, and what you would do differently, you get important clues about your marketing. Take notes of what you agree with in another's approach, and where you feel differently. These areas of difference are likely to be unique perspectives that your clients will resonate with. In a market where you are looking to stand out, you must know who's standing around you. Then you can find your unique voice among them.

My final thought on this is to ask you to broaden who you think of as competition. Notice above that I said others who meet the same needs as you do, not others who do the same thing as what you do. Why? Because in today's economy, there are multiple ways to get the same needs met. Someone experiencing an illness 100 years ago in the U.S. could go to the local doctor or treat it at home. Now in most places in the U.S., you can choose between a traditional or naturopathic doctor, a clinic, a herbalist, acupuncturist, or natural energy healer. There are multiple people whose different services could help you with your illness. In my business of marketing, there are consultants and coaches who specialize in marketing, along with business coaches and consultants who also deal with marketing—as well as books, online courses, and workshops that all offer marketing help. To differentiate yourself effectively in the mind of your potential customer, you need to look at a variety of options they could use and understand how you are different and the same from each of them.

Questions for Reflection:

- Do you resist looking at your competition?
- Can you imagine learning and growing from doing so?
- How could you reframe this to be more positive if you find it distasteful?
- Could you use studying your competition as a way to energize your own approach?

Find Your Resources

You are creating a marketing plan for your business—not a list detailing dozens of marketing activities you must enact by yourself. Too often, that's exactly how it feels, which can be a lonely and limited position.

Instead, look for all the resources available to you. Stretch beyond your own personal skill-sets or resources, and this will expand how much your business can deliver. Imagine what you could do with the right strategic partnerships or resources above and beyond yours. Increase the impact you make by becoming a part of a larger professional community. Ask the universe to show you the resources available to you in order to accomplish more. Don't feel like your business is all on you. It's not.

Your plan doesn't only involve you and your customers. In truth, your business came here to do something beyond you. Yes, it's your business, and maybe it's being run by you. Or maybe you are the inventor of or main service provider in it. Yes, it's terribly personal, but it's not really all about you. You and your business are separate entities, each with your own energy and desires.

Your marketing plan should name where your business wants to go in terms of visibility. Your job is finding the resources—money, people, and opportunities—for it to have that level of visibility. This takes the situation out of the limited I of the business person and into the greatest potential of the business.

Your marketing plan should go where your business wants to go. It's your role to take you both there

---

What if you and your business have different ideas about what kind of visibility your business should have? In my experience, it's best to let the business guide this. We tend to cloud our marketing plans with hopes, fears, and what we believe our financial needs to be. Our business usually has a clearer vision that's connected to our big why. In truth, we are all here to make a contribution and enact our why, and often our entrepreneurial activities are part of that ride, rather than the material one. But most of us can't get over our human thoughts about money when it comes to our business.

Even if at first there's a sizable difference, more often than not, the entrepreneur's view on visibility and their business's views on visibility come together at some point. Great, now you both want the same thing! It's usually only the timing that is different. Either the business wants a high level of visibility that seems scary for the entrepreneur at this time of their life, or the business wants to coast along at a time the entrepreneur believes it should be growing. I believe you'd do well to follow the lead of your business and trust in a higher universal order at play, even if it seems personally uncomfortable.

Besides, we don't always see what's happening at the time it's happening. Have you ever experienced a period in your life that seemed fallow or stagnant, only later to realize you were

AN AUTHENTIC MARKETING PLAN

gaining the exact skill-set you needed in order to take a giant step forward in your life?

Nancy was an art buyer who had great skill in her craft, and whose clients loved her work. But the projects were not coming in routinely enough for her business to feel stable. She experienced times of overwhelm when she had too many projects, and fear when there was too little work, causing her to scramble for more. Although she loved her business, she longed for it to grow into something both comfortable to her schedule and financial needs. Then she was invited to bid for a bigger project than she had yet had. This meant she had to hire some outside help to put the proposal together, and assemble a larger internal team than she was used to putting on her projects. Then, during the process of bidding for this job, her admin person let her know she was going to quit, one of the consultants she brought in for the internal team fainted during the proposal presentation and had to go to the hospital, and Nancy herself got into a car accident. To top it off, she wasn't awarded the large job.

Although this seemed like just the opposite of what she needed, it started her down the path of getting to the business she wanted. In the aftermath of everything that had happened, Nancy had to take back the tasks her admin was doing and set them up in a way that worked for her, rather than how her assistant had wanted to do them. She began learning every aspect of her business. In doing so, she realized she could do more if she upgraded her project management skills. So she took a course to become certified in this. She hired a bookkeeper and set up internal systems. Her business became more solid and streamlined.

When she realized she was uncomfortable with creating

relationships with strangers, she started attending more networking and social events. Taking this small risk over and over, she became more comfortable with her own value and how she is received by others. She went through every aspect of her professional and personal finances, cutting and organizing until she felt comfortable with what was coming in and going out. She could now discuss them and make decisions around them.

Although she didn't have enough work coming in, and the future of her business was uncertain, Nancy focused on getting comfortable with the reality of her current business, her skillset, and her desires for more business. This led her to find the courage to invest money in her business, hire outside help to refresh her website, and pursue new business opportunities, rather than waiting for them to find her. A few months later, Nancy had not only enough business again, but more than she'd had the year before. The biggest difference was Nancy achieved what she'd longed for—a business that worked comfortably with both her schedule and financial needs. She now feels comfortable with the notion that she can continue getting new business at a pace supportive to her because her business is set up to do that.

Did Nancy do all of this consciously? Not really. As these events were unfolding, she couldn't really see things were headed toward a good end. Did she love taking back the admin tasks, hiring a bookkeeper, or setting up new internal systems? Nope. But it seemed like the only reasonable choice. She could pack it all up, citing bad luck as a cause for her business failing, or take a step in a direction that felt personally uncomfortable. By showing up and taking the next step her business was asking her to take even though she didn't always love it, she lived her way into a more solid, confident version

AN AUTHENTIC MARKETING PLAN

of herself and, hence, her business.

What step is your business asking you to take? Are you willing to take it and trust the higher order that might be at play? Or are you sitting in your version of what should happen and asking your business, and perhaps, even the world, to shift around you? I see entrepreneurs doing both, though only one of these paths reliably works in the long run.

Just how do you find what level of visibility your business wants? Simply put, ask! That's right; your business loves to share its viewpoints and ideas with you, if you ask it. Since most of us aren't exactly in the habit of chatting it up with our businesses daily, here are a couple of tips on how to get in contact with your business's point of view.

1. **Free writing:** You may have heard of stream of consciousness writing in which you put your pen down on the paper and don't lift it for some period to get to the deeper wisdom you are holding inside yourself. You can use this same concept to get in touch with your business. It's helpful if you make a pleasant setting for yourself, perhaps in nature, or lighting a candle at your desk, or finding another beautiful setting to write in. This signals a special or sacred time. Take a few breaths and let go of any need to be in control or any fears you have about receiving new information. It's helpful if you can set aside any thoughts you have and write from a state of innocent curiosity. If you try to write from an anxious, controlling place, you will have a harder time. Choose the amount of time you are willing to write. I find 10 minutes to be a minimum, but over 20 minutes to be tiring. You can experiment to see what works for you. Ask yourself what your business has to say to you. Set the timer, then put your pen on the paper or hands on the keyboard, and write anything that comes up in your mind. I mean anything, so long as you don't stop writing. If you start thinking about the laundry,

ask yourself what your business perspective might be on that and write it. If you are thinking how silly this effort seems, ask your business what it has to say about that. Try to accept anything that comes up and get it all out on paper with the hope that you can begin to have a dialogue with your business. It might take a time or two of trying before your business (or the part of you that can tap into the spirit of your business) feels safe enough to say something real. After all, you've likely been ignoring it for some number of years now.

2. **Visualization:** The following is a visualization I created to tap into the same information. If you prefer to listen to it, either read through it while recording it and play it back for yourself, or download it here: lindabasso.com/theauthenticmarketer

> *Find a comfortable seated position. Feel the surface beneath your legs, what your feet are touching, and notice the position of your back. Lengthen through your spine so that your head and neck come over your hips, without your head or your shoulders slumping forward. Resting comfortably, imagine a golden light surrounding you, bringing you a deep sense of peace and acceptance. Breathe in this light, letting it infuse every cell in your body. Bathed in this loving light, imagine your business is now sitting across from you in its own chair. For even though your business seems to be yours, and may be of you, it is also separate from you. Your business has come to be in this time with its own agenda, its own ideas, and its own contribution that it wants to make. You are in partnership together on this journey. If you can approach a conversation with your business with curiosity and non-judgment, it can share with you what it needs to grow or make the contribution it wants to. First, ask your business what contribution it wants to focus on making in the coming year. Or, you can ask about next week. Pick a*

time you are curious about. Listen as your business tells you or shows you pictures, or communicates in some way to you about the contribution it wants to make, and by whom this contribution is being received. [pause] If you didn't receive anything, relax and be willing to allow this information to come in. Take whatever comes without judging it. Or, trust that it will reveal itself at another time. Now ask your business what level of visibility it wants to have to be able to make this contribution. Again, listen to what your business has to say, or the pictures it shows you, or however it wants to communicate this information to you. Allow the information to unfold naturally and easily. Perhaps you have a small level of visibility, only working with a limited number of people. If so, know that it is totally fine. Or perhaps you see yourself working with hundreds of people over the life of your business. Maybe thousands. Whatever you see or hear, know that all's well. [pause] If you notice any discomfort in yourself in receiving this information, be willing to set it aside for now. This can be dealt with at another time. When your business has shared the visibility it desires with you, thank it for sharing. Let it know that you will visit it regularly to check in and share information. Become aware of your physical body again. Notice your feet on the floor, your legs on the chair, and the position of your back. Come out of the visualization slowly, and open your eyes when ready.

Now that you have an idea of the kind of visibility your business desires, it's up to you to support it. If you are responsible for creating the visibility your business wants, just how do you find the resources for that? You need to tap into resources beyond the financial ones you need to have in place to enact your plan. Look at the people you know, the networks you are part of, vendors available to you, and even technology solutions. Yes, getting your business going in the right direction rests a lot on you, but not totally. Any successful person has a slew of people behind them supporting them. It's helpful if you create clarity for yourself, as most people are amazed by the amount of resources they really have in their lives. Go through the list below and note what you have resources for and what you do not. You want to know what support you have, and what may be missing to move forward gracefully.

What if you are lacking support in one or more areas? No problem! In coaching we call this upgrading your network. It means you consciously seek out anything missing from your professional resource pool, so that you have the right support in order to reach your business goals. That does not mean you're going to gain all the skills that are lacking for yourself. Let me repeat: this does not mean you are adding a long list of skills you must learn to your to-do list. It does mean making connections with the people who can provide them, or can refer you to those who can. A strong professional network means you can get done what you need to get done by resourcing from trusted professionals you've gathered around you.

No one moves forward without support behind them

Having a strong professional network can be the lifeblood of your business. When you see business owners who get most of their work by referral, you are likely looking at a business owner with a strong network of connections around them. We still live in an economy of people who choose to work with people they like and trust. Trust comes from nurturing strong relationships. It's not just about getting business. It's also about better serving your clients. When you are a well-

AN AUTHENTIC MARKETING PLAN

connected person, you have the possibility of helping your clients get whatever they need to be successful. When you can refer a client to a vendor to help them in their personal or professional life, or another person who can help them in some way, you are being of service to them.

Here's a list of categories to review on the amount of resources in your life. Put a check mark in two places—whether you have it or don't, and then whether it has to come from you or you can outsource it to another person. Download a printable version here: lindabasso.com/authenticmarketer

YOUR SELF

	Have	Don't Have	Has To Be You	Need Someone
Ideas for your business				
Strengths to enact ideas				
Personal talents & skills				
Health & energy				
Appearance/clothing				

PHYSICAL

	Have	Don't Have	Has To Be You	Need Someone
Office or place to work				
Storage or filing spaces				
Equipment (like a massage table or other)				
A well ordered home to support your off time				

THE AUTHENTIC MARKETER

SPIRITUAL

	Have	Don't Have	Has To Be You	Need Someone
Self-practice				
Sacred spaces				
Natural places				

NETWORK

	Have	Don't Have	Has To Be You	Need Someone
Professional connections				
Greater community				
Ongoing opportunities to meet new people				

FINANCE

	Have	Don't Have	Has To Be You	Need Someone
Budgeting skills				
Money tracking system				
Cash flow understanding				
Time for reviewing $				
Comfort with earning money				
Invoicing system				
Bill paying system				
Credit to get you through tight cash flow				
Savings to support you through downtimes				

AN AUTHENTIC MARKETING PLAN

RELATIONSHIPS

	Have	Don't Have	Has To Be You	Need Someone
Family harmony				
Close friends				
Close colleagues				

TECHNOLOGY

	Have	Don't Have	Has To Be You	Need Someone
Equipment (computer, printer, etc.)				
Writing/editing software (like Word or Pages)				
Presentation software (like Power Point or Canva)				
Systems to support business functions (appointment software, calendar program, online ordering, etc.)				
Website				
LinkedIn profile				
Facebook, Instagram, and other social media accounts				

Voila! Go back through the list and for anything you checked "don't have," you now know something you need to begin developing as a resource for your business. Here are ways you can expand your resource pool:

1. First, use the previous list to determine what kind of upgrades you need to make that you checked in the column

"Has to Be You." Then plan to get that upgrade into your life. If it's a skill-building upgrade, like learning a new software or how to budget, and you determine that you need this skill upgrade, ask around for classes, books, or teachers who can help you gain these skills—or look online. Set aside time in your schedule to learn the skills or make the upgrades that you need to make.

2. If you have upgrades that you checked in the column "Need Someone" as another person can make them for you, get busy hiring them. For example, maybe you want to dress more professionally or expand your creativity. Look for a coach or stylist who can help you achieve this. Or maybe you need to hire someone to create some systems for you.

3. If you need to expand your network so that you know more vendors or have more professional contacts, seek out appropriate networking groups. You can find them via online searches, through your Chamber of Commerce, or through Meetup.com. Some are drop-in groups you can go to now and then. Others require a weekly commitment. All of them let you visit a couple of times before you make any decisions. If you don't find a group near you, consider starting one! I've known several entrepreneurs who increased their business by starting their own networking group.

Your networking does not have to be limited to physical groups, although I recommend that every entrepreneur have strong ties to their community. You can participate in online networking in a couple of ways. One is through LinkedIn, which is an online network for the most part. I say for the most part because in truth, LinkedIn works best when you invite in only professionals you know in person when you start your profile, and regularly add new professionals you meet in the physical world. Knowing each of your connections personally means you have a know-like-trust factor with them and are more likely to respond to each other if a need arises. Everyone hates to have a stranger invite them to their circle only to have them start trying to sell them something! Likewise, when a friend or colleague of ours reaches out to be introduced to someone, we are usually all too happy to help. Create a profile, and invite every professional contact you personally know to connect with you via LinkedIn. Remember, these should be people you personally have met; otherwise it won't be effective. You can then interact with people in your LinkedIn network the same way you would in your physical networking groups. Say congratulations to them when they experience work success, send them an interesting article you just read, and regularly publish articles on your own expertise. Your goal should be to create the same level of visibility within your group as you might within your physical networking groups. LinkedIn then makes it easy to reach out to your network—and beyond—when you want to be introduced to someone or need something specific. For example, if you are doing research for a new service you're creating, you could search for people to have an informational interview with. When you find an ideal person, you can see if any of your connections are connected to that person so that they can facilitate a direct introduction to that person.

Another way you can network online comes from joining various Facebook groups that have your ideal clients in them or are filled with the types of professionals you need to know. By regularly commenting and sharing within these groups, you can create online connections similar to how you might create personal ones.

4. Now that you've created the awareness of what you need, be on the lookout for the universe to send it your way. This means be out and about! Talk to people sitting next to you in the café or at the gym. Ask people questions when

they seem to have what you are seeking. There's a world of resource around you if you are open to it coming to you. You can also use online searches and read books or articles to know more about topics you need to be savvy about. This rarely gets entirely solved while you sit in your office. Get involved in the world around you, and experience the amazing synchronicities that unfold.

Ask the Right People

Entrepreneurs ask me questions all the time. Politely, I point out that I could give my opinion, but that, unless I fit the profile of their perfect client, I might not be the right person to answer their question. Most pause as they consider my subtle clue, but choose to pursue their question anyway. We are often so hungry for advice in the beginning of our businesses that we ask anyone. Later, we are so wary of having received so much wrong input that we don't ask enough. Instead, try to find a balance of taking in and making your own way—and developing the discernment to know the difference.

Be sure to ask for input only from experts who jibe with your ideas about what a successful business really looks like and/or have ideologies and perspectives you respect. Often we take advice from anyone who's successful, only to discover the way that person earned their success doesn't match how we work. That experience becomes one of those learning experiences we all have had along the way. Or when we're having a bad day, reframed as wasted time and money.

I remember studying with one business coach for almost a year before realizing the model she taught was not one I ever wanted to have in my business. I went all the way through her program, even enacted a lot of what she taught with success. It wasn't until I sat down and mapped out how the next two years of my business would be if I used her model that I realized how unhappy I would be having that kind of business. Additionally, I realized over that year how hard she was working and what her business required of her just to keep up. Although she had skills valuable to me, she was not the right person to help me take my business where I wanted it to go, because she had no experience with the kind of business I wanted to have. Since then, I've chosen my teachers, mentors, and coaches with more care and understanding of what they could teach me, and how that plugs into growing my business.

It's important that you are careful about both the kind of people and the kind of advice you look for. When you think about your own business and where you want it to end up, ask yourself:

- Are the teachers and mentors in your world running businesses you admire, both in the service they provide and how they market it?
- Do you like the lifestyle they have?
- Do you agree with their ethics and approach?
- Do you hire coaches because they can teach you a specific skill you've already determined you need or because you became excited by their inspiring speech at a conference?

Asking people who fit the profile of your ideal client is a great way to get feedback related to your product or service, your marketing, how you deliver it, and how your customer service comes across.

I don't mean asking your current clients, even if they fit the description of your ideal client. You are already in a relationship with them, and they already hired you. This means they've passed the psychological barrier of deciding you are a fit for them, and their input will tend to be biased toward understanding your messaging. In other words, they aren't very helpful in helping you get new people in! Speaking with folks who fit the profile of your client but are not your client can be a simple way to get input on how your messages are being understood, what their needs and hopes are, how they take in information, and what their current beliefs are about your industry.

What kinds of things do you ask them? Well, start by using them as a testing ground. If you are writing an e-book, have a few testers read it and answer a couple of questions, such as what they learned from it, if it made them want to know more, and if it inspired them to take next steps with your work (in other words, follow the call to action I know you put at the end of your e-book!). If you're launching a new service or product, interview a few people before you finalize it to be sure you're building a product/service that meets their needs. Later, have a few use it and share their feedback about what they liked and didn't like.

Any marketing messages you write can be shared with these folks before you launch them to your greater audience. Finding out beforehand whether your marketing creates a response or not sure beats sending out your campaign messages only to hear crickets in response. Ditto for delivery and customer service. Getting comments on how that experience came across for testers and making adjustments feels better than hearing from a customer who's had a bad experience. Using people who fit *your* ideal client profile to preview your materials will help you be sure that what you are creating will be well received.

Of course, I'm not saying you should never ask your actual customers for their input. I encourage you to elicit feedback several times during your interactions with customers to be sure things are on the right track and they are happy. Also, ask them for a testimonial about their experience with you for use in your marketing materials. Ask them to review their experience via a survey or by answering a few questions when you finish working with them. This kind of information gathering will help you make the needed adjustments to your business so that it continues to flourish.

Celebrate Your Plan

If you've taken in the information in this section, then you know all you need to create a plan in your own way. You have identified your larger dream, your authentic goals, and named the amount you need to earn. You're aware of yourself and know the resources you have, as well as the ones you need to find. You've studied the market and gotten input from the right people.

Once you gather all this information, what do you do with it? It's time to move from gathering it to incorporating it into your plan. You'll need to review the information you receive, and use it to make decisions that are in alignment with your business goals. All the information either gets rejected or incorporated. And if it's included, that means acting on it. Too often I meet entrepreneurs who've been busy gathering information from various experts and customers—but never enact any of it. If your clients are giving you feedback that they want something from you, find a way to give it to them. If you seek an expert's advice, decide whether you should act on it and, if so, find the courage to do it. Remember, this is about living your marketing, not trying to do what you think you're "supposed" to do. Step into laying out what you are going to do, when you're going to do it, and whom you are going to do it with.

When you're done with your research, you have all the information you need to plan in this way. If you've been drawing conclusions about all the information you've been gathering, you can already see that. If not, carve out some time to reflect on what you've learned about each of these areas. Pencil out your reflections into a plan or paint them into a visual rendition. Or sticky note them all over your wall. It's not important what format you use. Remember, a marketing plan is like all the other plans you make in your life. It's simply what you're going to do, at what time, and with whom to end up where you want to be. If you still cannot see what your plan could be, talk with someone who can help you organize your thoughts. You just might need some help in crafting your plan into a digestible format.

Your plan can be as simple as jotting down a few notes about what you are going to do and when on a single piece of paper. Or, if you prefer, make it more elaborate. There's no shortage of templates on the internet. If you are a visual person, you can create a collage or piece of art reflecting on the information you've gathered—from a single vision board-style plan to an elaborate collaged notebook or box. There's no limit to how you can put your plan together, nor is there any right way. The formal business plans of many pages you've likely read about are primarily for companies needing to pitch investors for funding. If you aren't looking for funding, then you can do whatever you'd like.

There are some structural ideas to consider in creating your plan:

- **Less is more:** most of us can only accomplish about 3 goals per quarter (a quarter is ¼ of the year or 3 months). Yes, I know it seems like there are many, many things for you to do in your business, but you will get more done if you simplify. Focus on doing only two things in your business: serving your clients and getting your three big goals done. Of course, each of your three big goals will have many parts to them. There will be plenty to do! But it can aid in your decision-making and keep things from becoming overwhelming. If it's not

AN AUTHENTIC MARKETING PLAN

related to finishing up one of your big goals, it's a "no" for now. This can keep you from chasing every new thing and getting nothing done!

- **Tie your goals to your real desires.** So far we've looked at your purpose, your why, your heart's desire and your truth as means for understanding what you authentically want. Don't abandon yourself now and toss in goals that don't fit you. Find goals that are inspiring and exciting to reach. But also be sure they will move you toward your bigger dreams. In chapter three we looked at the big dream you have for your business. Any planning and goal setting you do now should move you toward this end goal for your business, not set you down another path.
- **Review every quarter.** Your plan won't help you if you never refer to it. Why do all that planning and toss it into a drawer? Choose a format you can use often, review every quarter, and update easily. Let it be an alive thing for you rather than feeling like dead weight. This kind of reflection and planning is what is meant when it's suggested that you work "on" your business in addition to working "in" your business. A good plan that you review and update is a powerful tool to fast forward movement. I use a one-page plan with my clients. You can download it here: lindabasso.com/authenticmarketer

Questions for Reflection:

- Are you willing to pull together all you've learned into a marketing plan for yourself?
- If you lack clarity in some area, how can you get the information you need to create this clarity?
- Is there anything else in the way of you making your plan? How will you deal with it?

CONCLUSION

To have the things we truly want, we have to grow into being our authentic selves. I wish it were different, that we could simply dream our perfect business and home life into being, but I've yet to see that happen. It takes courage, openness, determination, and action. The best laid plans never come to be if they don't get acted on. Am I right? How many times have you intended to do something, or longed to do something, or seriously wanted something to change, but you didn't actually get to the acting part—and it never happened?

I know because I've been there. My first career lasted almost 20 years, and I didn't love it. All along the way, I wanted to make a change, but I just couldn't see how. Good news for me in that, even though I wasn't yet making a change, I was doing some of the work in this book such as finding my truth, sussing out my purpose, and breaking family ties. That laid the groundwork so that when I finally saw my real opportunity—to reach thousands of entrepreneurs through my writing and speaking—I was finally able to start acting.

Now, powerful actions are part of my everyday vocabulary. That doesn't mean my days are filled with only sunshine

CONCLUSION

and roses. I constantly have to find ways to inspire myself, to take actions when I'd rather not, and support myself as I work through fears and doubts. Because here's the rub: no matter how far you've come, there's somewhere up ahead beckoning you to come further still. And then, the whole journey starts over again.

The trick is to learn to dance with cycles of wanting, growing, having, wanting more, and doing it again. I've learned that small, steady steps toward change are better than a big leap resulting in a lot of stress that makes you want to give up.

I hope this book has helped you in this process. Now that you've read it through, go back and pick an issue to move along a bit more. If you did only some of the exercises, do a few more. Take a look at your business and be honest about where you are struggling. Use the advice in this book to address this area directly. On any given day, open the book randomly, and see if the message applies to a situation within your business.

Steady, small steps forward add up over time to be big, lasting accomplishments

---

For effective change, you may need to live some of this material, then revisit it and have a new experience. You may find yourself drawn to new paths of exploration or compelled to dive more deeply into a concept. Again, trust your path. There's no exact formula for marketing, for business, or for life. There's only the process of it unfolding, and our decision to be conscious and engaged with the process. That's the path of authenticity.

Be kind to yourself along the way. I've made many significant changes in my life, but if I'm honest, the ones that stick are the ones that unfolded over a long period with small, subtle changes that added up over time to be a big change.

I hope this book has uplifted your thinking around marketing. And in my heart of hearts, I hope you are poised to go deeper than just reading the book. Take action. Step further into your truth, or out of your comfort zone and into a plan that's full of opportunity. Maybe you will cut some old ties and find a fresh perspective on being visible. All in all, I hope you begin to bring your whole self to your business.

This, in the end, brings you to your authenticity.

Isn't that the point? We know we have to either keep going, or pack it in and give up. It's simply not possible to just sit in the middle for any great length of time. If we can find tools for moving forward with more grace and ease, we can loosen up and enjoy the ride.

Good thing you don't have to go it alone. When you partner with the various aspects of yourself in this journey, you're held by an incredible wisdom that's all contained within. You get just the right amount of push, as well as the gentle hand of slowing you down, and all on an as-needed basis. When you step more fully into yourself, the universe steps in to hold the overall picture, so that you can relax into your current place with more ease. You can breathe a sigh of relief knowing it's not all up to you. You can step into this amazing opportunity we have as humans to bring all of ourselves out here on planet Earth. There's no better place to do that than in your business.

You don't even have to labor over how exactly you need to grow. I've seen many entrepreneurs pursuing endless growth programs, hoping they'll gain enough self-confidence, enough skill, or enough of something they lack that will ensure success. In truth, the right growth for you will come as you start to act in your business. It's a magic formula. There's no amount of getting ready you can do before acting in your business that will make sure it all works out. You learn by doing it.

The exact actions and growth we need are pointed out

CONCLUSION

by stepping forward. This is the best marketing advice I can offer—move forward in your business, trusting that you will be asked to grow in just the right way to ensure your success. I've seen this work so often that I've stopped being surprised, though I still feel awed by the miracle every time I see my clients grow to their next level.

The exact growth you need to excel in your business comes up as soon as you step forward—but not before

---

In the process, you'll learn some of what makes you tick. You'll accept more and more of who you really are. Knowing yourself brings you one of the most precious gifts you could receive. Once you accept where and who you are, you are freed up to rejoice in what a fabulous creation you are. That's when the fun starts.

It all comes back to this one idea—grow yourself, grow your business.

What's Next?

The channeling for this book contained the information I have shared here, plus much more. In the first three months, I received about 20,000 words of channeled material. By the time I explained all the concepts, added in examples and exercises, it grew to 110,000 words, which by a modern-day reader's standards, is simply too long. In addition, I knew that marketing can quickly feel overwhelming. Having a thick, heavy book just didn't feel right.

After some furious head-scratching, my editorial team and I decided to break the material up. Suddenly, I was publishing not one, but three books. Please consider sharing your opinion on Amazon as a review or recommending this first book to a fellow entrepreneur who might grow from reading it, and dive into the second and third books of this series. In these other two books, you'll learn how to love and laugh your way through marketing. With the support of these two powerful concepts, you'll drop the idea of marketing as only pursuing an endless to-do list and see that your marketing journey can be uplifting and supportive of making a real contribution in your work.

All the books are part of The Authentic Marketer series. This first book is called Live. The second book, Love, shows that when you offer your business efforts to something higher than yourself, you bring universal power to your approach. Rather than push your marketing out in the traditional way, Love shows you how to create resonance and divine timing within your marketing. You'll find that love helps you release resistance with blessings and become the creator you were meant to be. By truly hearing the stirrings of your own heart, releasing the drama of human life and getting to know yourself, you are one step closer to this path. There are questions for reflection, exercises, and instructions for rituals included. The third book, Laugh, takes you on a different path. You'll learn how powerful laughter can be. It heals and helps us to live better lives. Why not choose laughter over hard work? Then you can bring play into your marketing, which brings ease—and better results. This new lightness lets you step into flow within your business and your marketing, learning to experiment and refine your way to marketing success.

Again, you don't have to do it all alone. Not only can you access your authentic guidance on this journey, you can also join other like-minded entrepreneurs. Believe me, it's easier when we see that others are on a similar path. Too often we feel like the reluctance is only happening to us. I promise you it's not. Come find out how to join others on this journey at lindabasso.com/authenticmarketer. Together we can do this

CONCLUSION

much more easily than each of us on our own.

In the end, marketing is just one step in the journey. When you speak with successful entrepreneurs, they tell you about the thousands of steps they've taken to reach where they are. As growthful gals, we are all in a process that takes our entire lives to live out. Along the way, we become more and more of our best selves, which means we have more to contribute to others who may be just behind us on the path. Go on, get out there and grow yourself, so that you can share it with the world. I'll be right beside you doing the same.

EXCERPT FROM THE NEXT BOOK
The Authentic Marketer
Book Two: Love

"To love is to risk: being truly seen, being received and held, being heartbroken. It is a profoundly rich, raw place. Many of you have been practicing this in your relationships. Now you get to enact the same level of care, commitment, and participation in your business lives. It's deeply fulfilling, inspiring and heart filling." – channeled quote

We talk a lot about love. Movies, songs, greeting cards, even chocolate, espouse love—but as a culture we have very little exploration of what love really means. Too often "love" songs are about possession or infatuation. Romantic novels go toward either silliness or high drama. Hollywood promises a formula that rarely works in real life. True love promises to hold us forever—if only we could find it.

In contrast, real love means tending to something as if its growth was of utmost importance—similar to being a parent concerned for the movement of the child through each stage of its growth. This is true for all the loves in our lives, including our love to parents, partners, and friendships. This means love sometimes looks unloving when we have to have difficult, truthful conversations or hold boundaries, or have discipline in our reactions. Contrary to what Hollywood would have us believe, real love runs the gamut from happy to heartbreaking.

We think romantic love makes us complete, but in reality, that is more about getting our needs met and is not strictly related to love. Love is more about care and stewardship than it is romanticism. This is why old couples endure because they have surpassed surface notions of romance for the deeper currents of witnessing, tending, and holding, which ironically foster a deep sense of romance.

Think of love from within the spiritual or religious tradition you are part of or grew up. Is it portrayed as the passionate, romantic notion that we see in Hollywood movies? No. It's often parental, patient, and sacrificial—as in letting go in order to reach something higher. If you are growing into a new place, you usually have to leave the place where you are. Consider the hero's journey. When you read these stories in spiritual passages or about people being led through the desert, that doesn't seem scary. But you would likely balk if that happened within your own life. We cling to ideas that we can keep everything we have, be comfortable and reap the riches of more. It doesn't usually go this way.

To be successful in your business, you must be willing to redefine your definition of love. When you can pour this more patient and wise version of devotion over your business you will see dramatic results.

Loving your business means tending to it through the stage it's in, not demanding it be in the stage you want it to be in

---

For your business, this means that you develop fierce and tender notions of stewarding it through stages. This is different from looking at it for what it can provide you. You must seek to know each of the stages and devote the resources to see it through each of them. This is why bigger businesses often do well faster. They have a dispassionate view of the business that lends itself to tending these growth stages. On the contrary, many solopreneurs are passionately involved in their businesses. Passion is not love.

Let's take a look at these stages and what loving your business looks like through each.

- In the startup phase, love for your business does resemble the passionate Hollywood story a little bit. You feel driven to do something and pursue it with fervor. You are willing to give it almost everything and often act as if you will stick with it no matter what it costs. Or you behave like those dramatic people in a movie that say they want love one minute and at the slightest little snag threaten to walk away the next. Love here looks like learning to ride the ups and downs, enjoying it when it's good and not getting too discouraged when it's not. It's about developing the trust that you and this business can become something together.

- If you make it through the starting stage, you move onto the growth stage. Here you nurture your little sprout of a business to become a full grown plant. This means riding through a ton of developmental changes. If you are a parent, have a garden or have had a pet since it was small, you can understand my meaning. One stage of development gives way to the next and the next and the next. Sometimes it's all you can do to hang on at all. It demands more of your time and energy than you thought possible. This stage calls out the best and worst of you. Love in this stage is about you and the business both growing into bigger, better versions of yourself.

- Finally, you arrive at the mature business stage. This is the part where if you let it, the business and you can enjoy your success and grow old together. This stage can offer you some security and relief as the business can provide well with less of your time. It's also the time that the infatuation is over, the excitement can wane, and you either decide to drop in and commit or move onto the next startup. Love here is all about the conscious growth of maturation.

Why We Need Love in Marketing

You might find it odd that marketing and love are being put together. After all, marketing is often associated with something slightly distasteful at best and terrible or slimy at worst. Why in the world would we bring notions of love into such a bawdy place? Well, as is often the case, the answer is in the problem.

Whether you prefer to hear The Beatle's *All You Need Is Love* or Alicia Key's *Show Me Love*, we all intuitively agree on the importance of love. Why? Because love is the most powerful force there is. Period. There is no problem that exists that cannot be solved by pouring love on it. It may take time but in the end, love can heal anything.

So the question should really be flipped to: why wouldn't you approach marketing with love?

Love is definitely needed in the parts of our businesses that cause us stress and fear. Marketing, sales, technology, and finances spring to mind. Am I right? What part of your business causes dread? Is it working with clients you love? Bringing your gifts to the world? Getting to do what you want to all day long? Probably not. But bring up marketing or sales and I bet fear—or something worse— rears its head. Or think about the technology upgrades or financial assessments you need to do and you feel vaguely tired. The only real solution for stress or dread is love.

Why? From an energetic standpoint, you have two choices in reaction to something: to allow it, or not allow it. It's basically like stepping toward something and letting it be around you, or walking away from it and rejecting it being around you. Toward or away. Step toward something and want it around you, and you'll generally begin to feel positive emotions. If you do the work to court it, like any good relationship, it will nourish you back. Step away from it and paradoxically, it will cause havoc in your world. Avoiding the things you don't care for in your business doesn't make it easier; it makes it more of a struggle.

So love it is then. But how do we pour it on our marketing? It's not enough to just think of our visibility efforts fondly or to have gratitude for the new clients that come in. There are some deeper efforts that will unfurl the winds of fulfillment within our business if we let it. The following chapters offer ideas for loving approaches to your marketing.

***

Want to read more? If you'd like to be notified when **Book Two: Love** is available, sign-up here: lindabasso.com/authenticmarketernext

ENDNOTES

[1] Baumeister, Roy & Leary, Mark. (1995). The Need to Belong: Desire for Interpersonal Attachments as a Fundamental Human Motivation. Psychological bulletin. 117. 497-529. 10.1037/0033-2909.117.3.497

[2] Over H. 2016 The Origins of Belonging: Social Motivation in Infants and Young Children. Phil. Trans. R. Soc. B 371:20150072. http://dx.doi.org/10.1098/rstb.2015.0072

[3] Baumeister, Roy & Leary, Mark. (1995). The Need to Belong: Desire for Interpersonal Attachments as a Fundamental Human Motivation. Psychological bulletin. 117. 497-529. 10.1037/0033-2909.117.3.497

[4] Legault, Lisa. (2016). The Need for Autonomy. Encyclopedia of Personality and Individual Differences. 10.1007/978-3-319-28099-8_1120-1

[5] Legault, Lisa. (2016). The Need for Autonomy. Encyclopedia of Personality and Individual Differences. 10.1007/978-3-319-28099-8_1120-1

[6] https://news.stanford.edu/news/2013/february/talking-to-baby-021213.html

[7] White, Lawrence T. "Is Cognitive Dissonance Universal?" Psychology Today, Sussex Publishers, 28 June 2013, www.psychologytoday.com/blog/culture-conscious/201306/is-cognitive-dissonance-universal

[8] Newman, Kira M. "Six Ways Happiness Is Good for Your Health." Greater Good, 28 July 2015, greatergood.berkeley.edu/article/item/six_ways_happiness_is_good_for_your_health

[9] Fredrickson, Barbara, The broaden-and-build theory of positive emotions. (Philosophical Transactions of the Royal Society B: Biological Sciences. August 2004)

[10] Guven, Cahit. "Go on, Give Society a Break and Be Happy, but Not Too Happy, Deakin Economist Says." Deakin University Australia, 13 June 2011, www.deakin.edu.au/about-deakin/media-releases/articles/2011/go-on,-give-society-a-break-and-be-happy,-but-not-too-happy,-deakin-economist-says

[11] Silny, June What's So Great About Happiness, Anyway? (The Answer: Plenty!) Happify Daily, http://www.happify.com/hd/whats-so-great-about-happiness/

[12] Fredrickson, Barbara, The broaden-and-build theory of positive emotions. (Philosophical Transactions of the Royal Society B: Biological Sciences. August 2004)

Acknowledgements

My deepest gratitude to my developmental editor, Lynda McDaniels…thank you for shaping my ramblings and offering your unwavering optimism that there was something here. Your work helped me believe this could really happen.

Thank you Fay Thompson of Big Moose Publishing for your quick responses and taking this project through its last step.

To my amazing clients who impress and inspire me weekly. You keep me growing and humble me with your courage. Thank you for letting me share your stories.

My dear community and friends, thank you for patiently inquiring how my book was going and listening to me about it for these years.

Santiago, mi vida, I cannot put into words how much your ongoing support and acceptance means to me and my journey. I love you.

To my intelligent, warm, and humorous children Kayden and Alena—you are my greatest joy and source of growth.

And finally, thank you to Sonoma county for being this special place to live. The beauty and abundance around me is a source of replenishment for my soul.

Join The Authentic Marketer Community

Now that you've read the book, take it a step further.

Join Linda Basso and her community in exploring the topics within The Authentic Marketer in private coaching, online classes and online support groups. It's so much easier to step into being ourselves when we are in community, rather than going it alone.
Hope to see you there!

lindabasso.com/authenticmarketer
facebook.com/lindabassomarketingcoach

www.ingramcontent.com/pod-product-compliance
Lightning Source LLC
Chambersburg PA
CBHW071237070526
44583CB00017B/2218